Make It Easy,
Cupcake!

Make It Easy, Cupcake!

FABULOUSLY FUN CREATIONS IN 4 SIMPLE STEPS

Karen Tack AND
Alan Richardson

St. Martin's Griffin
New York

www.stmartins.com

The Library of Congress Cataloging-in-Publication Data is available upon request.

ISBN 978-1-250-13939-9 (trade paperback)
ISBN 978-1-250-13940-5 (ebook)

Our books may be purchased in bulk for promotional, educational, or business use. Please contact your local bookseller or the Macmillan Corporate and Premium Sales Department at 1-800-221-7945, extension 5442, or by email at MacmillanSpecialMarkets@macmillan.com.

First Edition: June 2018

10 9 8 7 6 5 4 3 2 1

To Kirk
A brother, a sculptor,
an inspiration

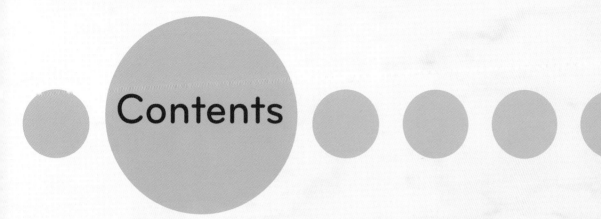

Contents

Introduction

Easy as 1-2-3-4

Ever wish you could just follow photos and not need to read a recipe? *Make It Easy, Cupcake!* does exactly that. Each eye-popping cupcake design has four simple photos that show precisely how we made them. And we've even added our personal tips to the photos to make it easier! (Of course, if you have any questions, the full recipe is right there on the page for you to read, too.)

In *Make It Easy, Cupcake!* we are up to our usual trickery, turning ordinary candy and snacks into over-the-top cupcake masterpieces. But this time we've included big colorful illustrations with labels that reveal every candy and snack used—so you can see exactly how to make them. It's a blast just looking at the photos to see how many parts you can identify for yourself!

Our easiest techniques make these cupcakes simply spectacular! We show you how to smash sugar into frosting to magically transform a cupcake into a sparkling Ballerina, Glitter Fairy, or Unicorn, and how your microwave can be used to create gorgeous Pink Magnolias and Cherry Blossoms. We'll even show you dozens of ways to turn ordinary cookies into Barking Dogs, Lucky Kitties, Chipmunks, Delivery Trucks, Football Players, and more.

Holiday decorating gets the "Make It Easy" treatment, too, with everything from gorgeous Valentine's Day Hearts to Santa and his Reindeer. There's even an elegant Christmas Village!

Now it's time to turn you into a *candy crafter!* It's simple—just grab a few everyday tools and a handful of grocery store candy, and when in doubt, always remember to make it easy, cupcake!

EVERYDAY CANDY BASH

Candyful cupcakes for events big and small!

CANDY-DROIDS

Pocky stick

Mallomar

M&M

orange slice

Mike and Ikes

mini M&M's

pearl

foil baking cup

Smart Cookie Choices!

SnackWell's

Whippet

mini chocolate-glazed doughnut

chocolate-coated Little Bites Fudge Brownie

CANDY ROBOT CUPCAKES

18 vanilla cupcakes, chilled
1 cup white decorating sugar
9 orange fruit slice candies
2 (16-ounce) cans vanilla frosting
18 chocolate Pocky sticks
18 Mallowmars, or your chocolate cookie choice
18 brown M&M's
½ cup M&M's Minis
36 Mike and Ike candies
18 colorful pearls, such as SweetWorks

1. Sprinkle your work surface with decorating sugar to prevent sticking. Roll out each orange slice to a 3¼-inch diameter round. Cut out two 1½-inch circles from each flattened candy to make 18 circles.
2. Spoon ¼ cup of the frosting into a zip-top bag. Spread the top of the cupcakes with a mound of the remaining frosting and smooth. Place an orange candy circle on top and press it into the frosting. Roll the tops in a bowl filled with the sugar to coat. Gently pat to reshape. Brush excess sugar from the orange candy circle.
3. Cut ¾ inch from the coated end of the Pocky sticks, discarding the longer pieces. Snip a small corner from the bag of frosting. Pipe a dot of frosting on the top and one side of each Mallowmar. Attach the cut end of a Pocky stick to the top dot and a brown M&M to the side dot.
4. Pipe a small dot of frosting on top of each cupcake and attach the heads. Add dots to the front and sides of the cupcakes to attach the M&M's Minis for the buttons, the pearl for the light, and the Mike and Ike candies for the arms.

Makes 18

1 Make orange circles

roll in sugar

use cookie cutter

flatten orange slice

2 Sugarcoat

decorating sugar

orange circle

mound frosting

3 Build head

frosting

M&M

Pocky stick

4 Assemble

Mike and Ike arm

mini M&M button

pearl light

7

BACKYARD BBQ

chocolate frosting

jelly beans

yellow frosting

breadstick

frosting

green apple twists

cupcake tops

pink frosting

red fruit leather

sesame seeds

cupcake top

sweetened coconut

orange- and green-tinted coconut

frosting

melted chocolate frosting

cornflakes

9

BAKED BEANS

Vanilla cake mix batter, prepared according to
  package directions
1 cup milk chocolate frosting
2 tablespoons light corn syrup, such as Karo
1½ cups orange jelly beans, such as Jelly Belly

1. Line a 12-cup cupcake tin with paper liners. Fill the cupcake liners halfway with the cake batter. Bake for 11 to 14 minutes, until the cupcakes are golden and a toothpick inserted into the center comes out clean. (The cupcakes will bake up short, leaving a slight lip to hold the beans.) Transfer to a wire rack and cool completely. Freeze the cupcakes for 30 minutes before assembly.
2. Combine the frosting and the corn syrup in a medium bowl. Microwave the mixture in 5-second intervals, stirring after each, until melted.
3. Add the jelly beans to the warm chocolate mixture and stir to coat evenly.
4. Spoon a heaping tablespoon of the jelly bean mixture onto the top of a cupcake and spread it to the edge of the liner. Repeat with the remaining cupcakes.

Makes 12 cupcakes

1 Bake short cupcakes

fill liner halfway with batter

leave paper lip exposed

2 Make sauce

milk chocolate frosting

light corn syrup

microwave to melt

Sauce the beans

3

orange beans

thinned sauce

4 Serve the beans

don't spill the beans

HOT DOGS

12 vanilla cupcakes, chilled
12 plain breadsticks, such as Stella D'oro
1 (16-ounce) can vanilla frosting
1 tablespoon chocolate frosting
Red and yellow food coloring, such as McCormick
1 piece green apple licorice, such as Kenny's Candy
   Juicy Twists

1. For the hot dogs, use a small serrated knife to saw 1¾ inches from each end of the breadsticks; discard the centers and reserve the ends. Put ¾ cup of the vanilla frosting in a small bowl and stir in the chocolate frosting and about 15 drops of red food coloring to tint the vanilla frosting brownish-pink. Microwave the tinted frosting in 5-second increments, stirring after each, until smooth. Line a cookie sheet with waxed paper. Coat each breadstick end with the frosting, allowing the excess to drip back into the bowl, and transfer to the lined cookie sheet. Refrigerate until set, about 15 minutes.

2. For the hot dog buns, use a small serrated knife to level the tops of the cupcakes with their paper liners. Make two parallel cuts in the top, ½ inch apart, and discard the center strips.

3. For the mustard, put 3 tablespoons of the vanilla frosting in a small bowl, tint it yellow with food coloring, and spoon it into a zip-top bag. Set aside. Spread a layer of the remaining untinted vanilla frosting on top of the trimmed cupcakes and smooth. Use the tines of a fork to gently score the edge of the frosting, pulling it to the center, to resemble the edge of a paper plate.

4. To assemble, place 2 coated breadsticks cut end to cut end on top of the cupcakes to make the hot dog. Cut one corner from the bag of yellow frosting and pipe a zigzag line of the frosting on the hot dogs as the mustard. Place a trimmed cupcake top on either side of the hot dogs, cut-side down, as the buns. Snip the green apple twists into small pieces and add as the relish.

Makes 12 cupcakes

Coat hot dogs

1

saw breadsticks

discard center

microwave frosting to melt

dip rounded ends

Trim bun

2

remove cupcake top at paper edge

parallel cuts

discard center

Score plate edge

3

use fork to mark frosting

pull into center

Assemble hot dog

4

add buns

frosting mustard

green licorice relish

13

SLIDERS

12 vanilla cupcakes, chilled
1 tablespoon sesame seeds
2 cups cornflakes
1 (.75-ounce) roll strawberry fruit leather, such as
  Fruit by the Foot
    1 (16-ounce) can chocolate frosting
    1 tablespoon light corn syrup, such as Karo

1. Sprinkle the tops of the cupcakes with sesame seeds, pressing lightly to adhere. Use a small serrated knife to level the tops of the cupcakes with their paper liners; set the tops aside.
2. Place the cornflakes in a bowl. Snip the red fruit leather into ¼-inch pieces and toss with the cornflakes.
3. Put ¾ cup of the chocolate frosting and the corn syrup in a small bowl and microwave until softened. Pour the frosting over the cereal mixture, tossing to coat completely.
4. Spread some of the remaining chocolate frosting on top of the cupcakes. Add a heaping tablespoon of the cornflake mixture, spreading it to the edge. Place the cupcake tops over the filling as the bun.

Makes 12 cupcakes

14

1 Trim bun

add sesame seeds

use serrated knife

trim at liner edge

2 Mix meat

toss with cereal

snip fruit leather

3 Add BBQ sauce

microwave frosting to soften

coat evenly

4 Assemble slider

meat mix

chocolate frosting

top with bun

15

COLESLAW

12 vanilla cupcakes, chilled
2 cups sweetened flaked coconut
Red, yellow, and green food coloring,
   such as McCormick
1 (16-ounce) can vanilla frosting

1. Set 3 tablespoons of the coconut aside and finely chop the remainder. Put 2 tablespoons of the chopped coconut into each of two separate bowls. Tint one bowl of coconut orange with the red and yellow food coloring and the second bowl light green with the green and yellow food coloring.

2. In a small bowl, mix ¼ cup of the vanilla frosting and 2 teaspoons water until smooth.

3. Combine the thinned frosting, the remaining untinted chopped coconut, and the unchopped coconut in a bowl. Toss until well blended. Sprinkle with the orange- and green-tinted coconut, tossing lightly to mix the colors.

4. Spread the top of the cupcakes with some of the remaining frosting and top with a mound of the coconut mixture to cover.

Makes 12 cupcakes

1 Tint veggies

yellow + red = carrots

yellow + green = parsley

chopped coconut

2 Make dressing

thin frosting with water

3 Lightly toss slaw

orange-tinted coconut

green-tinted coconut

untinted coconut

4 Serve up coleslaw

vanilla frosting

mound slaw

17

LEMONADE COOLERS

12 lemon cupcakes, chilled
1 (16-ounce) can vanilla frosting
4 yellow fruit slice candies
4 green fruit slice candies
Yellow food coloring, such as McCormick
12 yellow paper liners
4 wooden skewers
4 green thin bendy straws

1. Spoon ¼ cup of the frosting into a zip-top bag. Cut each fruit candy through the side, into 3 thin slices. For leaves, cut the green slices in half on an angle. For lemon slices, snip a small corner from the bag of frosting and pipe a line ⅛ inch from the rounded edge of each yellow slice to simulate the rind. Add 5 short lines to the center to mark the lemon sections.

2. Tint the remaining frosting yellow with the food coloring. Spread the top of the cupcakes with the yellow frosting and swirl. Place the frosted cupcakes in a yellow paper liner.

3. To assemble, stack two cupcakes with the additional paper liners and use the pointed end of a wooden skewer to make a hole in the center of the top cupcake and through the liners. Insert a trimmed skewer, about 3½ inches long, through the center of a third cupcake and its liners, and thread the skewer down through the hole in the stacked cupcakes to stabilize them. Repeat to make four stacks.

4. Add a lemon slice to the top of each cupcake stack, covering the hole from the skewer, and position 2 green leaves next to it. Cut each straw in half, keeping the bendy half. Garnish each cooler with a trimmed bent straw.

Makes 12 cupcakes

1 Slice fruit

three
thin
slices

lemon slice

leaves

frosting

2 Frost cupcakes

place in yellow liner

3 poke hole Stack coolers

stack

skewer

4 Add garnish

lemon

leaves
cover hole

snip straw
& insert

19

BLOOMIN' BEAUTIFUL!

pearls

green frosting

pink and white melting wafers

20

pink nonpareils

pink melting wafers

frosting

chocolate frosting

light blue frosting

21

PINK MAGNOLIA CUPCAKES

12 vanilla cupcakes, chilled
1 cup white melting wafers, such as Wilton
1 cup pink melting wafers, such as Wilton
Plastic teaspoons
Mini-cupcake paper liners
1 (16-ounce) can vanilla frosting
Red, green, and yellow food coloring,
   such as McCormick
3 tablespoons yellow pearls, such as SweetWorks

1. For the petals, put the white and pink melting wafers in separate small bowls, and microwave in 5-second intervals, stirring after each, until smooth. Combine the melted candies, stirring gently to keep swirls of separate colors. Line a cookie sheet with waxed paper. Dip the back side of a plastic spoon in the candy to coat, but do not go over the edge of the spoon. Place the spoon on the lined cookie sheet, candy-side up. Once the cookie sheet is filled, freeze the spoons for 5 minutes, until set. Gently remove the candy from the back of the spoon. Any broken pieces can be melted and used again. Repeat the process to make about 84 petals.

2. For the blossoms, reheat the remaining candy and spoon it into a zip-top bag. Snip a small corner from the bag. Pipe some candy into the bottom of a mini-cupcake paper liner. Arrange 4 petals in the liner, wide-end down in the melted candy, overlapping them slightly. Add 2 or 3 more petals in the center, using more melted candy to secure them if necessary. Refrigerate until set, about 10 minutes.

3. Put ¼ cup of the vanilla frosting in a small bowl and tint it pink with the food coloring, then spoon it into a zip-top bag. Snip a small corner from the bag. Pipe a dot of pink frosting into the center of the flower and add some yellow pearls to make the flower center.

4. Tint the remaining frosting bright green with the green and yellow food coloring. Frost the top of the cupcakes and smooth. Carefully remove the flowers from the paper liners and press one on top of each cupcake.

Makes 12 cupcakes

1 Make petals

dip back of spoon

pink & white melting wafers

do not cover edge

2 Assemble blossom

hardened petals

arrange in mini paper liner

melted candy

melted candy

3 Add center

pink frosting

yellow pearls

4 Attach blossoms

green frosting

23

CHERRY BLOSSOM CUPCAKES

13 chocolate cupcakes, chilled
1 (10-ounce) bag pink melting wafers, such as Wilton
Mini plastic cocktail spoons
1 cup chocolate frosting
1 (16-ounce) can vanilla frosting
Neon blue food coloring, such as McCormick
1 tablespoon pink nonpareils, such as Wilton

1. Line a jelly-roll pan with waxed paper. For the petals, put the pink melting wafers in a small bowl and microwave in 5-second intervals, stirring after each, until smooth. Spoon some of the melted candy into a zip-top bag. Snip a very small corner from the bag. Pipe the melted candy into the mini spoons, but do not fill them over the edge. Tap the spoons lightly to smooth the tops. Place the filled spoons on the lined jelly-roll pan, using the lip of the pan to support the spoon handles and keep the melted candy level. Refrigerate until the candy is set, about 5 minutes. Carefully remove the petals from the spoons; any broken petals can be melted and used again. Repeat to make about 75 petals.

2. Spoon the chocolate frosting into a zip-top bag and ¼ cup of the vanilla frosting into a separate bag. Tint the remaining vanilla frosting light blue with the food coloring. Frost the top of the cupcakes with the light blue frosting. Arrange the cupcakes on a serving platter in the desired branch shape. Snip a ¼-inch corner from the bag of chocolate frosting. Starting from a bottom corner of the cupcake assembly, pipe lines of chocolate frosting to form the main branch. Pipe more chocolate lines to thicken the branch and to create side branches.

3. Arrange 5 pink petals as a flower cluster along the branch on each cupcake, pointed ends out and overlapping slightly. For buds, place random single petals along the branches.

4. Snip a small corner from the bag with the vanilla frosting and pipe 5 or 6 short lines in the middle of each flower, pulling the frosting from the center out. Sprinkle the centers with pink nonpareils. Pipe a dot of chocolate frosting at the base of the buds.

Makes 13 cupcakes

1 Make petals

small cocktail spoons

rest on lip of pan

do not cover edge

chill to harden

2 Draw branches

cupcakes touching

overlapping lines

chocolate frosting

3 Add flowers

overlap slightly

hardened petal

pointed end out

4 Add centers

short strokes of frosting

nonpareils

MARSHMALLOW DAFFODILS

12 vanilla cupcakes, chilled
18 marshmallows
½ cup yellow decorating sugar, such as Cake Mate
12 large orange gumdrops
2 teaspoons white nonpareils, such as Wilton
1 (16-ounce) can vanilla frosting
Green and yellow food coloring, such as McCormick

1. For the petals, snip the marshmallows crosswise into 4 or 5 slices. Put the decorating sugar in a bowl and dip the marshmallow slices to coat.
2. For the centers, use a small melon baller or spoon to scoop out the flat side of the gumdrops. Sprinkle nonpareils inside the scooped opening.
3. Tint the frosting bright green with the green and yellow food coloring. Spread some frosting on top of the cupcakes and smooth. Arrange 6 marshmallow petals side by side, overlapping if necessary, around the perimeter of the cupcake, leaving a ¾-inch opening in the middle.
4. Place the gumdrop, scooped-side up, in the center of the petals, pressing into the frosting to secure.

Makes 12 cupcakes

1 Make petals

decorating sugar

coat sticky side

slice marshmallows

2 Scoop center

large gumdrop

nonpareils

small melon baller

sprinkle in hole

3 Shape blossom

green frosting

marshmallow petals

overlap edge

4 Add center

press into frosting

27

START YOUR ENGINES!

rrrrrr!

graham sticks

red melted candy

mini marshmallows

mini Oreo

marshmallow

M&M's

Twizzlers Pull'n'Peel

blue frosting

COOKIE BIPLANES

12 vanilla cupcakes, chilled
6 marshmallows
12 mini marshmallows, plus ¼ cup for clouds
36 graham sticks
½ cup white melting wafers, such as Wilton
1 (16-ounce) can vanilla frosting
Neon blue food coloring such as McCormick
6 Oreo Minis
3 strands red licorice lace, such as Twizzlers Pull'n'Peel
½ cup red melting wafers, such as Wilton
24 brown M&M's
12 yellow M&M's

1. Snip the large marshmallows in half crosswise. Snip 12 mini marshmallows into thirds crosswise.
2. Line a cookie sheet with waxed paper. For the top wing, trim ⅛ inch from one short end of 24 graham sticks and place the cookies in pairs, cut ends together, on the lined cookie sheet. Put the white melting wafers in a zip-top bag and microwave them in 5-second intervals, massaging the bag after each, until smooth. Snip a small corner from the bag. Pipe some melted candy on the cut ends of the graham sticks and press the paired cookies together. Refrigerate to set, about 5 minutes. For the bottom wing, cut the remaining graham sticks in half crosswise.
3. Separate the mini Oreos—remove and discard the creme center—to make 12 cookies. Tint the frosting blue with the food coloring. Frost the top of the cupcakes with the blue frosting. Place a large cut marshmallow on top, cut-side down, as the engine. Pipe a dot of melted candy on top of the marshmallow and add a mini cookie. Press a long graham stick wing into the frosting, using a dot of melted candy to secure the wing to the flat side of the marshmallow. Add 2 small bottom wings parallel to the top wing, about 1 inch apart, on the opposite side of the marshmallow, securing them with some melted candy.
4. Cut the red licorice into twenty-four 1½-inch pieces. Put the red melting wafers in a zip-top bag and microwave them in 5-second increments, massaging the bag after each, until smooth. Snip a small corner from the bag. Use dots of the melted red candy to attach the licorice between the ends of top wings and the point where the bottom wings meet the large marshmallow. Pipe lines of the red candy along the top edge of the wings. Add the brown M&M's as the wheels. Pipe a dot of white melted candy, reheating it if necessary, and attach 3 mini marshmallow pieces as the propeller and a yellow M&M nosepiece in the center. Arrange the remaining ¼ cup mini marshmallows as clouds.

Makes 12 cupcakes

1 Build engine

cut marshmallow in half

engine

engine

3 slices

propeller

cut mini marshmallows in thirds

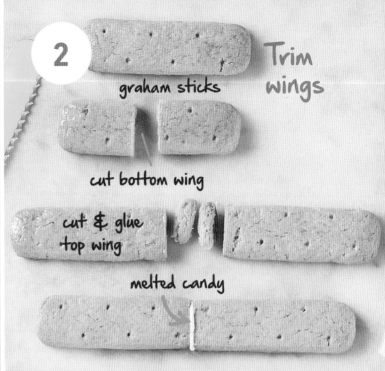

2 Trim wings

graham sticks

cut bottom wing

cut & glue top wing

melted candy

3 Attach wings

blue frosting

top wing

marshmallow engine

mini Oreo

melted candy

bottom wings

4 Add details

licorice lace

M&M nose

propeller

melted candy

M&M wheels

BEETLE BUGS

12 vanilla cupcakes, chilled
24 Oreos
4 blue licorice twists, such as Twizzlers
1 (16-ounce) can vanilla frosting
1 cup blue decorating sugar, such as Cake Mate
6 Vienna Fingers
6 flat square marshmallows, such as Jet-Puffed Stacker
  Mallows
24 yellow M&M's
12 yellow PEZ candies
12 blue M&M's Minis

1. For the wheels, use a small serrated knife to saw ⅛ inch from one edge of each Oreo. Saw the small trimmed pieces in half crosswise and remove the creme; use these pieces as the wipers. For the bumper, cut each licorice twist into three 2-inch pieces.

2. Spoon ¾ cup of the frosting into a zip-top bag. Spread some of the remaining frosting on top of each cupcake and smooth. Put the decorating sugar in a bowl and roll the tops of the cupcakes in the sugar to coat. Gently pat to reshape. For the car hoods, separate the Vienna Fingers—remove and discard the creme—to make 12 cookies. Snip a small corner from the bag of frosting. Pipe some frosting on top of a cookie to cover. Lightly press the coated cookies in the blue sugar to coat.

3. Pipe a dot of frosting on the lower half of the cupcakes and add the hood, sugar-side up. For the windshield, cut a marshmallow in half and use a dot of frosting to attach it with the cut side against the hood.

4. For the bumper, use a dot of frosting to attach the licorice piece on the lower half of the hood. For the headlights, pipe 2 dots of frosting on either side of the hood and push a yellow M&M into each dot. Attach the cookie wipers, a PEZ license plate, and a mini M&M hood ornament, using dots of frosting to secure each. For the wheels, place the Oreos cut-side down on either side of the cupcakes, under the hood.

Makes 12 cupcakes

Customize Your Car! Change the Color!

1 Auto parts

wheel

Oreo

bumper

wiper

Twizzlers

2 Sugarcoat

cupcake

frost

press in sugar

decorating sugar

Vienna Fingers

coat with frosting

3 Car assembly

cut marshmallow

window

hood

FISKARS

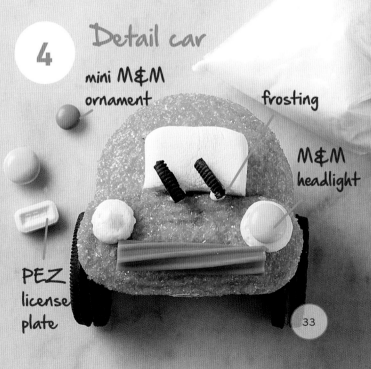

4 Detail car

mini M&M ornament

frosting

M&M headlight

PEZ license plate

33

SWAN LAKE

circus peanut

marshmallow

circus peanut

dark chocolate frosting

decorating sugar

candy-dipped pretzel

marshmallow

pink frosting

candy hearts

strawberry wafer

frosting

candy décors

edible glitter

MARSHMALLOW SWANS

12 vanilla cupcakes, chilled
9 circus peanuts
18 marshmallows
½ cup white decorating sugar
6 pretzel twists, such as Bachman
½ cup white melting wafers, such as Wilton
1 (16-ounce) can vanilla frosting
¼ cup dark chocolate frosting

1. Place the circus peanuts on their side and cut them in half lengthwise. For the feet, use pinking scissors to cut 12 of the flat slices in half on a slight angle. For the beaks, cut the remaining 6 slices in half crosswise. Trim each half into a ½-inch triangle.

2. Snip the large marshmallows in half on an angle. For the heads, remove a ½-inch piece from the pointed end of 12 of the marshmallow halves and add the candy beak to the sticky cut end. For the tails, snip a notch from the pointed end of the remaining 12 pieces. For the wings, snip 6 marshmallows crosswise into 4 slices each. Snip 2 notches from one short end of each wing. Put the decorating sugar in a bowl and dip the tails and wings in the sugar to coat.

3. Line a cookie sheet with waxed paper. For the necks, carefully break the loops from the pretzel twists. Put the melting wafers in a small microwave-safe bowl and microwave in 5-second intervals, stirring after each, until smooth. Dip the pretzel loops into the melted candy, allowing the excess to drip back into the bowl. Press the dipped loops in the decorating sugar to cover and transfer to the lined cookie sheet. Refrigerate until set, about 5 minutes. Spoon the dark chocolate frosting into a zip-top bag. Snip a small corner from the bag. Pipe some dark chocolate frosting around the wide end of the beaks and slightly up the sides of the face on the marshmallow.

4. Spread the top of the cupcakes with a mound of frosting and smooth. Press a tail, notched end up and pointing out, near one edge of each cupcake. Press one end of a pretzel neck into the frosting, curved side toward the tail. Add the marshmallow wings on either side of the neck, notched ends out. Add a circus peanut foot on either side of the tail, webbed toes out. Dip the flat cut side of each marshmallow head in the melted candy, reheating the candy if necessary, and attach the heads to the top of each pretzel neck, holding it in place until secure.

Makes 12 cupcakes

1 Make feet & beaks

circus peanut

slice

webbed feet

beak

pinking scissors

2 Shape heads & wings

diagonal cut

head

one notch in tail

slice

decorating sugar

wing

tail

two notches in wing

3 Cut & dip necks

neck

discard

melted candy

decorating sugar

chocolate

sugared neck

4 Assemble swan

press neck into frosting

mound frosting

37

STRAWBERRY BALLERINAS

12 strawberry cupcakes, chilled
12 strawberry wafer cookies
1 (16-ounce) can plus 1 cup vanilla frosting
Neon pink food coloring, such as McCormick
24 pink heart-shaped candies, such as SweetWorks
1 tablespoon pink and white candy décors, such as Cake Mate
2 tablespoons edible glitter, such as Wilton

1. For the torso, use a small serrated knife to saw the wafers crosswise to make twelve 2-inch pieces. Discard the smaller piece. Use a 1¼-inch round cookie cutter or knife to cut a ½-inch scoop from one short end of the 2-inch wafer pieces.

2. Put 1⅓ cups of the frosting in a bowl and tint it light pink with the food coloring. Spoon ½ cup of the pink frosting into a zip-top bag. Spoon the remaining vanilla frosting into a separate zip-top bag. Spread a thin layer of the remaining pink frosting on top of the cupcakes and smooth. Snip a small corner from each bag. For the tutu, start at the center and pipe tight loops of vanilla frosting to the edge of the cupcakes (it will look like flower petals). Pipe a second layer of smaller loops on top of and in between the first layer of loops.

3. Insert a torso, scooped-end up, into the center of the piped tutu, leaving 1½ inch of the wafer exposed. Using the pink frosting, pipe a solid line along the scooped end of the wafer and a decorative border around the base.

4. Use a dot of pink frosting to attach candy hearts, pointed end up, on either side of the scooped neck as the sleeves. Add the candy décors to the tutu and place a white décor at the center of the scooped neckline. Sprinkle the cupcakes with the edible glitter.

Makes 12 cupcakes

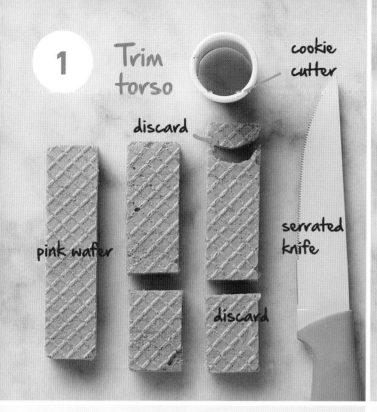

1 Trim torso

cookie cutter

discard

pink wafer

serrated knife

discard

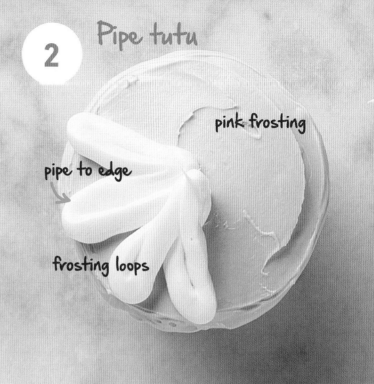

2 Pipe tutu

pink frosting

pipe to edge

frosting loops

3 Build ballerina

push torso into tutu

add details

pink frosting

4 Add sparkle

sleeve

edible glitter

candy heart

candy décors

39

BALLOON ART

gum squares

decorating sugar

licorice lace

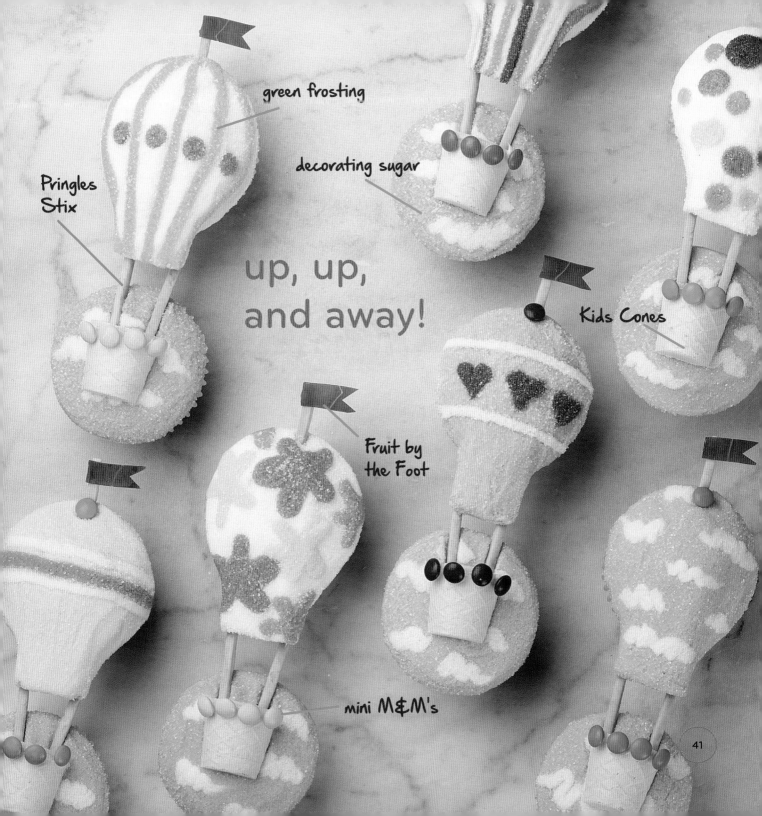

green frosting

decorating sugar

Pringles
Stix

up, up,
and away!

Kids Cones

Fruit by
the Foot

mini M&M's

41

PARTY BALLOONS

12 vanilla cupcakes, chilled
12 Lorna Doone shortbread cookies
1 (16-ounce) can vanilla frosting
48 small white gum squares, such as Chiclets
$^2/_3$ cup each red, green, blue, orange, and yellow
   decorating sugars, such as Cake Mate
12 black licorice laces

1. Use frosting to attach a Lorna Doone cookie to
   the top of each cupcake, flat-side up, allowing
   one cookie corner to hang over the edge. Put
   the cupcakes on a cookie sheet and freeze for 15
   minutes.
2. Spread a mound of the remaining frosting on top
   of the cookies and cupcakes and smooth into a
   balloon shape. Press 4 pieces of gum in a grid
   pattern, like a window reflection, on the upper
   right side of the frosted cupcakes. (Be sure the
   placement is the same on every cupcake.)
3. Put the decorating sugars in individual bowls. Roll
   the cupcake tops in the desired sugar color to coat.
   Gently pat to reshape. Brush any loose sugar from
   the gum pieces.
4. For the strings, use a toothpick to make a hole in
   the edge of each cupcake, under the cookie. Insert
   a piece of licorice into the hole.

Makes 12 cupcakes

1 Shape balloons

frosting

Lorna Doone

flat-side up

hang cookie off side

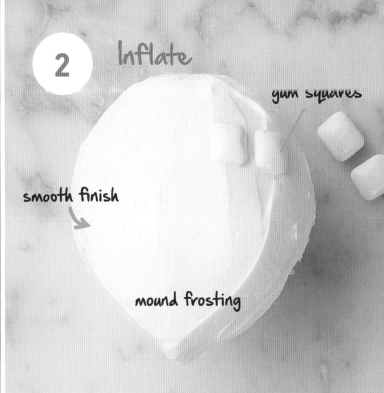

2 Inflate

gum squares

smooth finish

mound frosting

3 Sugarcoat

sugar sticks to frosting, not gum

decorating sugar

4 String balloons

insert licorice lace

poke hole

toothpick

43

HOT AIR BALLOONS

16 vanilla cupcakes, chilled
2 whole graham cracker sheets
½ cup white melting wafers, such as Wilton
8 Joy Kids Cones
4 inches strawberry fruit leather, such as
  Fruit by the Foot
10 Pringles Stix cookie sticks,
  any sweet flavor
2 (16-ounce) cans vanilla
  frosting
Pink, neon blue, red, green,
  and yellow food coloring,
  such as McCormick
1 cup white decorating
  sugar
¼ cup M&M's Minis

1. For the balloon cupcakes, use
   a small serrated knife to separate
   the graham crackers into quarters
   along the perforated lines. Put the
   melting wafers in a small bowl and
   microwave in 5-second increments,
   stirring after each, until smooth. Spread
   a thin layer of the melted candy on one
   side of the graham cracker pieces. Add
   more melted candy to a cupcake and
   attach a graham cracker, coated-
   side down, allowing 1 inch to
   overhang the edge. Repeat
   with 7 more cupcakes. Put the
   cupcakes on a cookie sheet
   and freeze them for
   15 minutes.
2. For the basket, use a small
   serrated knife to saw ¾ inch
   from the top edge of the
   cones and discard. Split the
   remaining base down the middle to make 2
   identical baskets. For the flag, cut the fruit leather
   crosswise into ½-inch pieces and cut a notch
   from one short end. Cut 2 cookie sticks into
   quarters; cut the remaining 8 sticks in half.
3. Put 3 tablespoons of the frosting into each of
   five small bowls. Tint them pink, blue, red, green,
   and yellow with the food coloring and transfer the
   tinted frostings to separate zip-top bags. Spoon
   ¼ cup of the remaining white frosting into a
   separate zip-top bag. Put 1 cup of the remaining
   white frosting in a small bowl and tint it light
   blue; cover and set aside for the clouds. For the
   balloon cupcakes, working on one cupcake at a
   time, spread a mound of the remaining white
   frosting on top of the cupcake and cookie, and
   smooth. Snip small corners from the bags
   of tinted frosting. Pipe vertical lines (or your
   own design) on top of each cupcake. Put the
   decorating sugar in a bowl and roll the tops of
   the cupcakes in the sugar to coat. Gently pat
   to reshape. For the cloud cupcakes, spread the
   top of the 8 remaining cupcakes with the light
   blue frosting. Snip a small corner from the bag
   of white frosting and pipe small squiggles of
   frosting on top. Roll the tops of the cupcakes in
   the decorating sugar to coat.
4. Arrange a balloon cupcake and a cloud cupcake
   about 1 inch apart on a serving plate or platter.
   Attach 2 long cookie sticks 1 inch apart under
   the base of the balloon, inserting them into the
   cupcake to secure, and rest the opposite ends
   on the cloud cupcake. Press the cone basket
   over the ends of the cookie sticks. Insert a
   small cookie stick piece at the top of the
   balloon cupcake. Pipe a dot of frosting on
   the stick and add a flag. Use frosting to
   attach mini M&M's to the rim of the basket
   and the base of the flag.

   Makes 16 cupcakes

1 Create shape

melted candy

coated cookie

graham crackers

overhang 1 inch

2 Make basket

trim Kids Cone

cut in half

fruit leather flag

Stix

FISKA

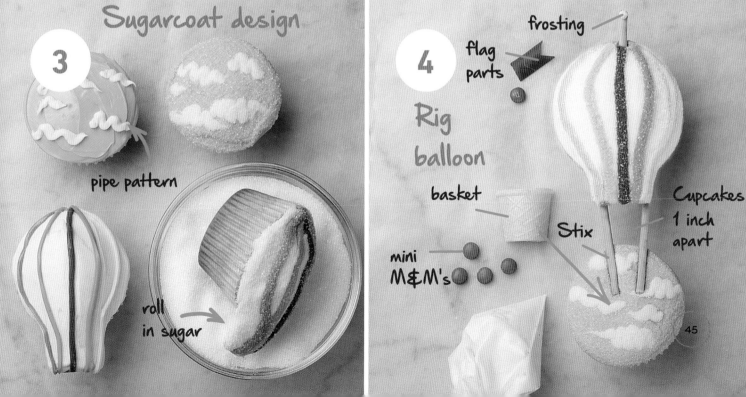

3 Sugarcoat design

pipe pattern

roll in sugar

4 Rig balloon

frosting

flag parts

basket

mini M&M's

Stix

Cupcakes 1 inch apart

45

HELMET
HEADS

Cheerios

decorating sugar

black pearls

Vienna Fingers

multicolor sprinkles

Tootsie Rolls

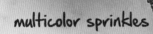

frosting

score!

pretzel sticks

black licorice laces

FOOTBALL SQUAD

12 vanilla cupcakes, chilled
3 Vienna Fingers
1 (16-ounce) can plus ½ cup vanilla frosting
Red and blue food coloring, such as McCormick
¾ cup each red and blue decorating sugar, such as Cake Mate
¼ cup dark chocolate frosting
24 black pearls, such as SweetWorks
6 O-shaped cereal pieces, such as Cheerios
2 strands black licorice lace

1. For the faces, separate the Vienna Fingers—remove and discard the creme—to make 6 cookies. Use a small serrated knife to saw each cookie in half crosswise to make 12 pieces.
2. For the helmets, divide the can of frosting between two bowls. Tint one bowl red and one bowl blue with the food coloring. Spoon 1 tablespoon of the red frosting into a zip-top bag and set aside. Put the red and blue decorating sugars in separate bowls. Spread a mound of the tinted frosting on top of a cupcake and smooth. Roll the top of the cupcake in the corresponding color sugar to coat. Gently pat to reshape. Repeat to make 6 red and 6 blue cupcakes.
3. Press a cookie piece, cut side near the center, into each sugar-coated cupcake, allowing ¼ inch of the cookie to overhang the edge, for the face. Sprinkle more sugar over any exposed frosting.
4. Spoon the remaining ½ cup vanilla frosting and dark chocolate frosting into separate zip-top bags. Snip small corners from the bags. For the eyes, pipe 2 white dots near the top of the cookie and add black pearls. Snip a small corner from the bag of red-tinted frosting and pipe a red mouth with any expression you prefer. Use a small serrated knife to saw the Cheerios in half. Attach one half with a dot of frosting for the nose. Use frosting to pipe white stripes and zigzags on top of the helmets. For the face guard, cut the black licorice into twenty-four 1¼-inch pieces. Pipe 2 dots of chocolate frosting on either side of the cookie face. Press the ends of 2 pieces of licorice into the frosting dots.

Makes 12 cupcakes

1 Make faces

separate cookie

remove filling

cut in half

Vienna Fingers

2 Sugarcoat

mound frosting

decorating sugar

3 Put on helmet

add sugar to exposed frosting

push face into frosting

4 Add game face

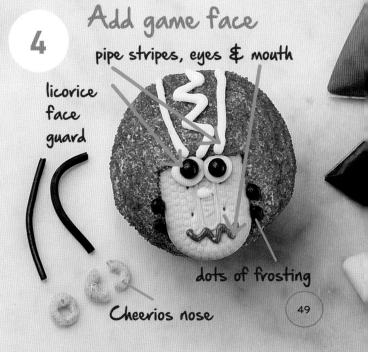

pipe stripes, eyes & mouth

licorice face guard

dots of frosting

Cheerios nose

49

GOAL POSTS

12 vanilla cupcakes, chilled
¼ cup light cocoa melting wafers, such as Wilton
48 thin pretzel sticks
12 small Tootsie Rolls
1 (16-ounce) can vanilla frosting
Green and yellow food coloring, such as McCormick
1 cup multicolored nonpareil sprinkles, such as Cake Mate

1. For the goal posts, put the melting wafers in a small bowl and microwave in 5-second increments, stirring after each, until smooth. Line a cookie sheet with waxed paper and arrange 4 pretzel sticks into a goal post shape (center post, crossbar, and two uprights) on the lined cookie sheet. Dip the bottom ends of the uprights in the melted candy and attach them to the ends of the crossbar. Dip the top end of the center post in the melted candy and attach it to the middle of the crossbar. Repeat to make 12 goal posts total. Refrigerate until set, about 5 minutes.

2. For the footballs, roll each Tootsie Roll into an oval shape with slightly pointed ends. Spoon ⅓ cup of the frosting into a zip-top bag. Snip a very small corner from the bag. Pipe a line down one side of the ball. Pipe three short lines across the first line to make the white laces.

3. Tint the remaining frosting bright green with the green and yellow food coloring. Spread the top of the cupcakes with some of the green frosting and smooth. Pipe 3 parallel white lines evenly spaced on top of the frosting. For the crowds, put the sprinkles in a bowl and dip opposite sides of the cupcakes into the sprinkles by about ½ inch, covering the ends of the lines.

4. To assemble, use a toothpick to make a small hole in the green frosting at one end of the field. Insert the goal post into the hole and add a football to the field.

Makes 12 cupcakes

50

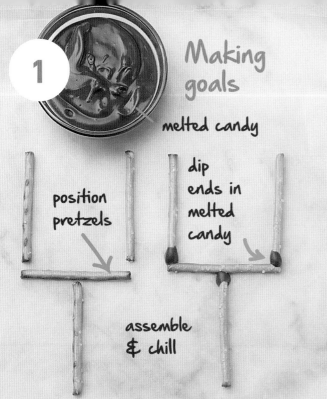

1 Making goals

melted candy

position pretzels

dip ends in melted candy

assemble & chill

2 Shape footballs

roll oval

pipe laces

pointed ends

vanilla frosting

3 Fill stadium

white stripes

cover ends of stripes

green frosting

multicolored sprinkles

4 Raise goal posts

toothpick

poke hole

insert pretzel

add football

SPECIAL DELIVERY!

mini vanilla wafer

black pearl

NECCO wafer

candy décor

circus peanut

Pringles potato chip

Pringles Stix

shimmer sugar

pink melting wafers

jumbo marshmallow

Pringles Stix

starlight candies

candy décor

frosting

mini M&M

decorating sugar

mini vanilla wafer

DELIVERY STORKS

12 vanilla cupcakes, chilled

1 cup pink, blue, or yellow melting wafers, such as Wilton

6 Pringles potato chips

36 Pringles Stix cookie sticks, any sweet flavor

2 circus peanuts

12 white NECCO wafers

1 (16-ounce) can vanilla frosting

12 black pearls, such as SweetWorks

1 cup white shimmer sugar, such as Cake Mate

1. Line a jelly-roll pan with waxed paper. Put the melting wafers in a small bowl and microwave in 5-second increments, stirring after each, until smooth. For the wing, snap the potato chips in half on an angle. Dip the cut edge of the chip into the melted candy to coat by about ⅛ inch. Transfer to the lined jelly-roll pan. For the neck and legs, dip the cookie sticks into the melted candy, leaving the end you are holding uncovered. Allow the excess candy to drip off back into the bowl. Place the sticks on the lined pan, with the uncoated end supported by the lip of the pan. Refrigerate until set, about 5 minutes.

2. For the beaks, cut the circus peanuts in half lengthwise. Cut six ½-inch-long triangles from each half. Spoon the remaining melted candy into a zip-top bag. Microwave to remelt, if necessary. Snip a small corner from the bag. Pipe a dot of melted candy on each NECCO Wafer and attach them to the coated end of 12 cookie sticks. Insert a beak into the melted candy, pointed end out, and let set. Spoon ¼ cup of the frosting into a zip-top bag. Snip a very small corner from the bag. Pipe a dot of frosting on each NECCO wafer and add a black pearl for the eyes.

3. Spread a mound of the remaining frosting on top of the cupcakes and smooth. Put the shimmer sugar in a bowl and roll the tops of the cupcakes in the sugar to coat. Gently pat to reshape.

4. To assemble, push the stick end of a head assembly into each cupcake at one edge. Cut about 1 inch from the uncoated ends of 2 of the remaining cookie sticks and insert the cut ends near the bottom edge of each cupcake as the legs. Insert the wide end of a wing into the frosting on top of each cupcake.

Makes 12 cupcakes

1 Dip body parts

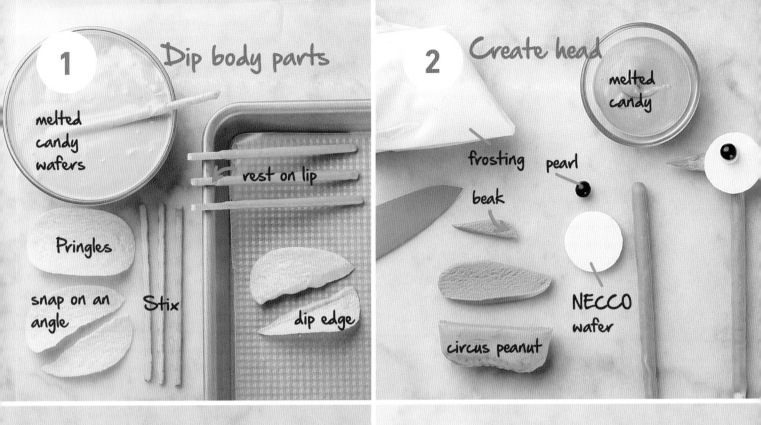

melted candy wafers

rest on lip

Pringles

Stix

snap on an angle

dip edge

2 Create head

melted candy

frosting

beak

pearl

NECCO wafer

circus peanut

3 Sugarcoat

mound frosting

shimmer sugar

4 Assemble stork

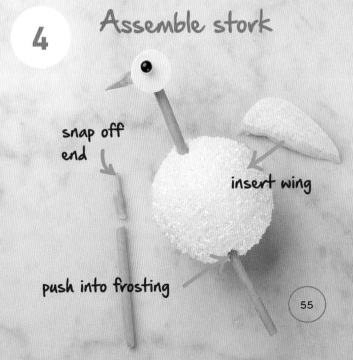

snap off end

insert wing

push into frosting

MARSHMALLOW BABY BUNDLES

12 vanilla cupcakes, chilled
6 jumbo marshmallows, such as Campfire
12 Pringles Stix cookie sticks, any sweet flavor
½ cup white melting wafers, such as Wilton
12 mini vanilla wafers, such as Nilla Wafers
1 (16-ounce) can vanilla frosting
¼ cup dark chocolate frosting
Neon blue food coloring, such as McCormick
12 small red heart décors, such as Wilton

1. For the baby bundles, snip the jumbo marshmallows in half crosswise. Reshape each half as a circle and place them cut-side down on a sheet of waxed paper. Snip a diagonal piece about 1 inch long from the upper right and upper left edges of each circle, with the cuts meeting at the top to create a teardrop shape. For the bundle ties, snip one of the trimmed pieces in half crosswise.

2. For the feet and neck, cut the Stix into thirds. Insert 2 pieces into the right cut side of the marshmallow and one piece into the left side, leaving about ¾ inch of each piece exposed.

3. Place the candy melts in a zip-top bag and microwave in 5-second intervals, massaging the bag after each, until smooth. Snip a small corner from the bag. For the ties, pipe a dot of melted candy at the pointed end of the bundle and attach 2 of the small pieces of marshmallow. Use a dot of candy to attach the vanilla wafer head to the single stick. Chill until set.

4. Spoon ¼ cup of the vanilla frosting into a zip-top bag and the dark chocolate frosting into a separate bag. Snip very small corners from the bags. Tint the remaining vanilla frosting light blue. Frost the top of the cupcakes with the blue frosting and smooth. Place the bundle assembly in the center of the cupcakes, pressing lightly to secure. Use the dark chocolate frosting to pipe eyelids on the vanilla wafer. Add a dot of vanilla frosting and attach the heart mouth. Pipe white lines as the folds in the bundle.

Makes 12 cupcakes

1 Shape bundle

cut in half →

jumbo marshmallow

trim each side

bundle

tie

2 Add neck & legs

Stix

3 pieces

insert in marshmallow

3 Add head & ties

vanilla wafer

melted candy

4 Make baby faces

chocolate frosting

pipe frosting pleats

candy décor mouth

BABY BUGGIES

12 vanilla cupcakes, chilled

1 (16-ounce) can vanilla frosting

2 tablespoons dark chocolate frosting

½ cup each pink, blue, and yellow coarse decorating sugar, such as Wilton

24 Pringles Stix cookie sticks, any sweet flavor

24 Starlight candies, any fruit flavor

12 to 18 mini vanilla wafers, such as Nilla Wafers

12 to 18 red heart décors, such as Wilton

12 colored M&M's Minis

1. Spoon ½ cup of the vanilla frosting into a zip-top bag and the dark chocolate frosting into a separate bag. Snip a small corner from the bags. Spread a mound of the remaining vanilla frosting on top of each cupcake and smooth. Put the decorating sugars in separate bowls and roll the tops of 4 cupcakes in each color sugar to coat. Gently pat to reshape. Put the cupcakes on a cookie sheet and freeze them for 15 minutes.

2. Using a small paring knife, make two cuts in the top of the cupcakes no deeper than the liner, one cut from the center to the top edge, and one cut from the center to the right edge. Insert the knife into the side of the cupcake level with the edge of the liner to loosen and remove the section of cake top between the two cuts. Pipe vanilla frosting on the exposed cake and smooth.

3. Cut 12 of the cookie sticks in half. For the wheel supports at the bottom of the buggies, insert 2 cut cookie sticks into the edge of each cupcake just above the liner, leaving ¾ inch exposed. Pipe vanilla frosting on top of the cookie sticks and add Starlight candies as wheels. For the handles, insert a whole cookie stick level with the liner, in the frosted area near the outside of the cupcake, and add a mini vanilla wafer next to it, as a head.

4. Use vanilla frosting to pipe a line of rickrack across the center of the buggies and add ribs to the bonnets. Pipe dark chocolate eyes on top of the vanilla wafers. Attach the heart mouths with a dot of vanilla frosting. Add a mini M&M button to each buggy canopy.

Makes 12 cupcakes

1 Sugarcoat buggy

mound frosting

decorating sugar

2 Create canopy

remove wedge

trim flush with liner

frost exposed cake

3 Add head, handle & wheels

mini vanilla wafer

Stix

frosting

starlight candies

wheel supports

4 Detail buggy

chocolate frosting

frosting

mini M&M

candy décor

59

JEEPERS, PEEPERS!

Kids Cones

chirp

jelly bean

Froot Loops

marshmallows

Spree

chocolate melting wafers

mini vanilla wafer

tweet

61

BIRD-WATCHERS

12 vanilla cupcakes, chilled
24 Joy Kids Cones
12 mini vanilla wafers, such as
 Nilla Wafers
¾ cup dark cocoa melting wafers, such as Wilton
12 marshmallows
1 (16-ounce) can vanilla frosting
Red and yellow food coloring, such as McCormick
24 purple Spree candies
12 pink jelly beans
2 cups Froot Loops cereal

1. For the binocular barrels, use a small serrated knife to
   saw ½ to ¾ inch from the base of each cone. (Make
   the cut straight or on an angle to alter the direction of
   the barrels, keeping them in pairs.) For the ears, saw
   the mini vanilla wafers in half. Line a cookie sheet with
   waxed paper. Put the melting wafers in a small bowl
   and microwave in 5-second increments, stirring after
   each, until smooth. Dip the wide end of the cones into
   the melted candy to coat by 1 inch. Allow the excess
   candy to drip off back into the bowl. Invert and place
   on the lined cookie sheet. Refrigerate until set, about
   5 minutes.
2. For the lens, snip the marshmallows crosswise into
   thirds; discard the center section and reserve the end
   pieces. Place one of the pieces in each cone,
   sticky-side in, inserting to just below the
   candy-coated edge.

Munchkin Fledgling page 64

3. Spoon ½ cup of the frosting into a zip-top bag. Tint the
   remaining frosting light peach with the red and yellow food
   coloring. Spread the peach frosting on top of the cupcakes
   and smooth. Press a pair of cones side by side, candy-coated
   side out, into the top of the cupcakes as the binoculars. Add
   the vanilla wafer ears, cut side into frosting, on either side. For
   the eyes, snip a small corner from the bag of white frosting,
   pipe a dot of frosting on top of the marshmallows, and attach
   a Spree candy for the eye.
4. For the nose, add a jelly bean below the binoculars. For the
   mouth, attach a red Froot Loop below the nose. Apply one
   color of Froot Loop hair, each styled differently, to the head of
   each birdwatcher.

Makes 12 cupcakes

1 Make eyepieces

trim cone

melted candy

mini vanilla wafer

ears

dip lip

2 Insert lenses

push into cone

snip marshmallow

dry side out

3 Add eyes & ears

press cones into frosting

dot of frosting

Spree eyes

4 Finish faces

cereal hair

jelly bean nose

cereal mouth

63

MUNCHKIN FLEDGLINGS

24 vanilla cupcakes, chilled

2 cups red, blue, or yellow melting wafers, such as Wilton

24 plain doughnut holes, such as Dunkin Munchkins

24 mini vanilla wafers, such as Nilla Wafers

48 yellow NECCO wafers

48 yellow or orange M&M's Minis

1 (16-ounce) can caramel frosting

3 cups sweetened flaked coconut, toasted

48 brown M&M's

24 red, blue, or yellow M&M's (to match the melting wafers)

48 yellow or orange M&M's

1. For the body, put the melting wafers in a small bowl and microwave in 5-second intervals, stirring after each, until smooth. Line a cookie sheet with waxed paper. Insert a toothpick into each doughnut hole and dip the doughnut holes into the melted candy to coat. Allow the excess candy to drip back into the bowl and transfer to the lined cookie sheet. For the wings, use a small serrated knife to saw the vanilla wafers in half. Dip the cut edge of the wafers into the melted candy and transfer to the lined pan. Refrigerate until set, about 5 minutes. Remove the toothpicks from the doughnut holes.

2. Spoon the remaining melted candy into a zip-top bag. Reheat if necessary. Snip a very small corner from the bag. For each bird, pipe dots of candy on the front of the coated doughnut hole and attach 2 NECCO wafers as the eyes. Use additional dots of candy to attach the cookie wings, candy-coated-side up, and 2 mini M&M's (yellow or orange) as the beak. Chill until set.

3. Spread the top of the cupcakes with a mound of caramel frosting. Put the toasted coconut in a bowl and roll the tops of the cupcakes in the coconut to cover.

4. Gently press a fledgling into the coconut nest on top of the cupcakes. Use a dot of melted candy to attach a brown M&M for the pupils and an M&M (match the color to melting wafers) as the top feather. Add M&M feet (yellow or orange) at the base of each bird.

Makes 24 cupcakes

1 Dip birds

doughnut hole

melted candy

toothpick

dip

mini vanilla wafer   dip edge

2 Face it & wing it

NECCO wafers

eye

beak

melted candy

melted candy

yellow mini M&M

3 Start nesting

mound caramel frosting

toasted coconut

4 Fledge the birds

eye

melted candy

M&M feather

feet

eye

65

KEEP ON TRUCKIN'

M&M

Tootsie
Fruit
Chews

Swedish fish

M&M's

fruit leather

circus peanuts

banana
Runts

Spree

Chiclet

Runts

66

Change the Candy Cargo!

marshmallow

Runts

sour belt

mini Oreo

Reese's mini peanut butter cups

sprinkles

Pocky

Froot Loops

graham crackers

Chiclets

frosting

67

DELIVERY TRUCKS

24 chocolate cupcakes, chilled

12 whole cinnamon graham cracker sheets

¾ cup light cocoa melting wafers, such as Wilton

1 (16-ounce) can dark chocolate frosting

36 Oreo Minis

½ cup vanilla frosting

1 cup M&M's

3 (6-ounce) boxes Runts

12 colored gum pieces, such as Chiclets

6 chocolate Pocky sticks

Optional: Additional Runts or other candies to create your favorite delivery truck (see previous spread)

1. Use a small serrated knife to saw the graham crackers in half crosswise along the perforated line to make 24 squares. Set aside 12 squares. Saw the remaining squares in half along the perforated line to make 24 rectangles. Shorten 12 of the rectangles by trimming ½ inch from one short end, and discard the small pieces.

2. Put the melting wafers in a small bowl and microwave in 5-second increments, stirring after each, until smooth. Spread some of the melted candy on the back of each cookie piece to keep them crisp. To assemble a cab, position a short rectangle vertically on top of one long rectangle while the candy is still wet, aligning them at either the right or left corner. Chill until set.

3. Spread the top of the cupcakes with the dark chocolate frosting and smooth. Arrange 2 cupcakes side by side on a plate or platter. Place a cab cookie assembly on the upper part of a cupcake and a trailer cookie behind the cab on the cupcake next to it, leaving room beneath both cookie pieces for the wheels. Press the mini Oreos into the frosting below the cookies as the 3 wheels. Repeat to make 12 trucks.

4. Spoon the vanilla frosting into a zip-top bag. Snip a small corner from the bag. For each truck, pipe dots of frosting as doorknobs and attach a yellow M&M as the headlight and matching color M&M's for the hub caps, the banana Runts as the fenders, and the Chiclets for the windows. Cut the Pocky sticks into 4 equal pieces each and add them as the exhaust and tailpipes. Pipe more frosting on the side of the trailer and add the Runts (or other candies) as the cargo signage.

Makes 24 cupcakes

1 Truck parts

discard

short rectangle

square trailer

long rectangle

2 Undercoating

melted candy

coat backsides

short rectangle

long rectangle

glue together with melted candy

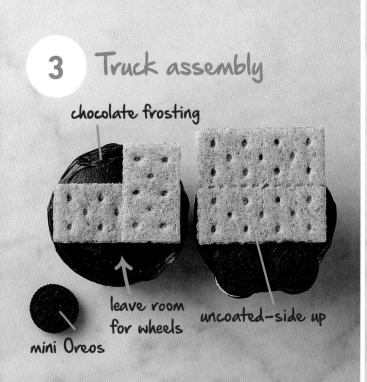

3 Truck assembly

chocolate frosting

leave room for wheels

uncoated-side up

mini Oreos

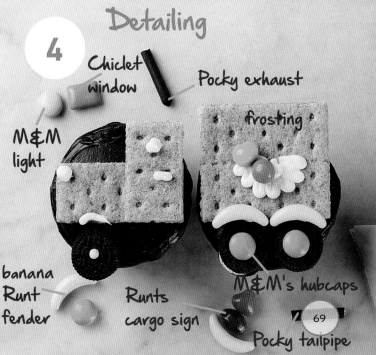

4 Detailing

Chiclet window

Pocky exhaust

M&M light

frosting

banana Runt fender

Runts cargo sign

M&M's hubcaps

Pocky tailpipe

69

MAKE-BELIEVE IT!

Bugle

pink decorating sugar

Nutter Butter

M&M

chocolate sprinkles

dark chocolate frosting

marshmallow

pink frosting

white melting wafers

mini vanilla wafers

chocolate frosting

yellow frosting

candy décor

Laffy Taffy

Juicy Fruit gum

edible glitter

mini vanilla wafers

PINK UNICORNS

12 vanilla cupcakes, chilled
6 Nutter Butter cookies
1 cup white melting wafers, such as Wilton
12 thin pretzel sticks
12 Bugles cone-shaped corn snacks
3 tablespoons pink decorating sugar, such as Cake Mate
1 (16-ounce) can vanilla frosting
1 cup white coarse decorating sugar, such as Wilton
3 marshmallows
Neon pink food coloring, such as McCormick
3 tablespoons chocolate frosting
12 brown M&M's
Chocolate sprinkles

1. Line a cookie sheet with waxed paper. For the heads, separate the Nutter Butters—remove and discard the filling—to make 12 cookies. Put the melting wafers in a small bowl and microwave in 5-second increments, stirring after each, until smooth. Dip the cookies in the melted candy to coat. Allow the excess candy to drip back into the bowl and transfer to the lined cookie sheet. Refrigerate until set, about 5 minutes.

2. For the horns, dip the tip of a pretzel stick into the melted candy and insert it into the opening of each Bugle. Holding the pretzel stick, dip the Bugles into the melted candy to cover. Allow the excess to drip back into the bowl. Put the pink decorating sugar in a bowl. Roll the Bugles in the sugar to coat. Transfer to the lined pan and refrigerate to set.

3. Spoon ¼ cup of the vanilla frosting into a zip-top bag. Frost the top of the cupcakes with some of the remaining vanilla frosting and smooth. Put the white decorating sugar in a bowl and roll the tops of the cupcakes in the sugar to coat. Gently pat to reshape. Snip a small corner from the bag of vanilla frosting. Pipe a dot of frosting to attach a coated cookie to each cupcake, allowing the cookie to hang slightly over the edge. Snip ¼ inch from each end of the marshmallows; keep the ends and discard the center. Snip the slices in half to make 12 ears. Press an ear behind each cookie, sticky side into the frosting, and insert the pretzel with the horn in front of the ear.

4. Put ¼ cup of the remaining vanilla frosting into each of two bowls. Tint one bowl pale pink and one bowl bright pink with the food coloring. Spoon the two pink frostings and the chocolate frosting into separate zip-top bags. Snip a small corner from the bags. For the eyes, pipe a dot of vanilla frosting and attach an M&M and 3 sprinkles for lashes. Pipe a white highlight on each M&M. Use the chocolate frosting to pipe a mouth and nostrils. Use the pink frostings to pipe the manes, alternating the two shades as desired.

Makes 12 cupcakes

1 Dip heads

separate cookie

remove filling

melted candy

coated cookie

2 Sugarcoat horns

melted candy

decorating sugar

Bugle & pretzel

3 Assemble

slice marshmallow ends

cut in half

ear

insert horn

sugarcoat cupcake

4 Add details

light pink

pipe mane

dark pink

pink frosting

add M&M eye

chocolate frosting

73

GLITTER FAIRIES

12 vanilla cupcakes, chilled
36 mini vanilla wafers, such as Nilla Wafers
24 yellow gum sticks, such as Juicy Fruit or gum of your
   choice
12 green, pink, or yellow Laffy Taffy
1 (16-ounce) can vanilla frosting
Yellow food coloring, such as McCormick
¼ cup dark chocolate frosting
½ cup white edible glitter, such as Wilton
12 pink mini heart décors, such as Cake Mate
12 thin pretzel sticks

1. For the arms and legs, use a small serrated knife to saw
   ⅓ inch from opposite sides of 24 mini wafers; discard the
   centers.
2. Make a diagonal cut in each piece of gum to remove ⅓
   of the stick. Trim all the pieces to curve the sides, making
   24 small wings and 24 large wings. For the tunics, cut two
   small notches from one short end of each piece of taffy.
   Cut a curve in the opposite end for the neckline.
3. Put ¼ cup of the frosting in a bowl and tint it bright yellow
   with the food coloring. Spoon the yellow frosting, ¼ cup
   of the vanilla frosting, and the chocolate frosting into
   separate zip-top bags. Tint the remaining vanilla frosting
   pale yellow. Spread the pale yellow frosting on top of the
   cupcakes and smooth. Sprinkle the outer edge of the
   cupcakes with some of the glitter. Pinch the taffy tunics
   in the middle to shape and place one on top of each
   cupcake. Pinch one end of each wing and add a large and
   small wing to either side of the tunics.
4. Snip small corners from the bags of frosting. Pipe yellow
   frosting hair on top of the whole vanilla wafers and sprinkle
   with glitter. Pipe eyes with the dark chocolate frosting and
   use a small dot of vanilla to attach the pink heart mouths.
   Insert a pretzel stick into the cupcakes at the curved end
   of the taffy, leaving ½ inch exposed. Pipe a dot of vanilla
   frosting on top of each pretzel and add a head. Use dots
   of frosting to attach the arms at the sides and the legs at
   the bottom of the tunics.

Makes 12 cupcakes

1 Cut arms & legs

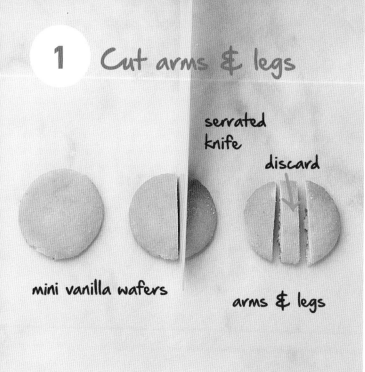

serrated knife

discard

mini vanilla wafers

arms & legs

2 Snip wings & body

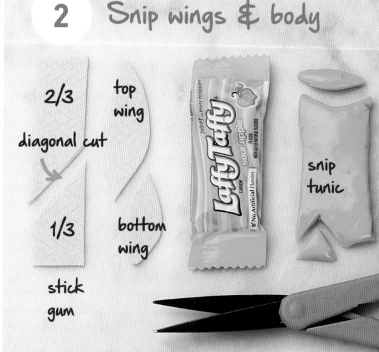

2/3 top wing

diagonal cut

1/3 bottom wing

stick gum

Laffy Taffy — sour apple

snip tunic

3 Assemble fairy

pinch taffy in middle

pinch gum at end

edible glitter

4 Finish fairy

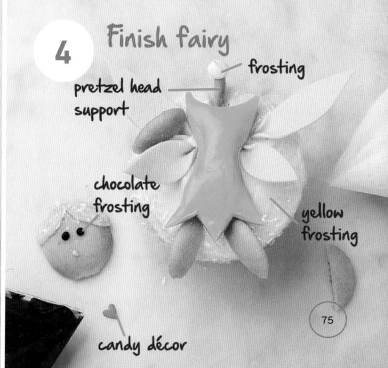

pretzel head support

frosting

chocolate frosting

yellow frosting

candy décor

75

NURSERY GAMES

spice drop

stick gum

candy décors

decorating
sugar

Dum Dum

colored straw

tinted frosting

mini M&M's

jelly bean

mini vanilla wafer

BABY BEARS

15 vanilla cupcakes, chilled
1 (16-ounce) can vanilla frosting
Red, yellow, green, and blue food coloring, such as McCormick
45 mini vanilla wafers
30 brown M&M's Minis
15 small jelly beans

1. Divide the frosting among five small bowls and tint each bowl a different pastel color: pink, blue, green, yellow, and orange. Spoon each color frosting into a separate zip-top bag. Snip a small corner from the bags. Working with one color of frosting, pipe 2 dots about 1 inch apart near the edge of the cupcakes and attach the vanilla wafers as the ears.
2. For the fur, pipe swirling lines of frosting around the outer edge of the ears and cupcakes.
3. Fill in with additional frosting swirls to completely cover the cupcakes and cookies. Repeat to make 3 cupcakes of each color.
4. For the features, position the cupcakes with the ears at the top, and lightly press a vanilla wafer on the bottom half, flat side down, as the muzzle. Add M&M eyes above the muzzle. Pipe a dot of frosting on the muzzle and attach a jelly bean nose to match the frosting color.

Makes 15 cupcakes

1 Attach ears

mini vanilla wafer

frosting

tinted
frosting

2 Start fur

pipe
outside
first

frosting loops

very small hole

3 Fur coat

completely cover with loops

4 Make faces

frosting

mini vanilla wafer

mini M&M eye

jelly bean nose

79

BABY RATTLES

12 vanilla cupcakes, chilled
24 inches orange, blue, pink, green, or yellow bubble
  gum tape or stick gum
1 (16-ounce) can vanilla frosting
1 cup orange, pink, yellow, green, or blue decorating
  sugar, such as Cake Mate
12 thin pretzel sticks
12 yellow spice drops
Candy décors, such as Cake Mate
12 light green thin straws
12 green, orange, yellow, blue, or pink Dum Dums
  lollipops

1. For the bows, cut the gum crosswise into twelve
   1¾-inch pieces and twelve ¼-inch pieces. Pinch the
   center of the larger pieces and wrap the smaller piece
   around the pinched area.
2. Spoon ¼ cup of the frosting into a zip-top bag.
   Spread a mound of the remaining frosting on top of
   each cupcake and smooth. Put the decorating sugar
   in a bowl and gently roll one edge of the cupcakes
   in the sugar to coat one-third of the top, keeping
   a straight line where the sugar meets the frosting.
   Gently pat to reshape.
3. Add candy décor polka dots to the exposed frosting
   of each cupcake. Insert a pretzel stick into the flat
   bottom of a spice drop. Snip a small corner from the
   bag of frosting. Pipe a dot of frosting at the center
   of the sugared area near the edge of the cupcakes.
   Insert a pretzel with a spice drop into the dot of the
   frosting as the rattle top.
4. For the handles, cut the straws into 4-inch lengths.
   Insert a straw on the edge of the cupcake opposite
   the spice drop, allowing 2¼ inches to overhang the
   edge. Use a dot of frosting to attach a bow over the
   hole made by the straws. Insert a Dum Dum stick into
   each straw.

Makes 12 cupcakes

1 Tie bow

gum tape

cut shapes

pinch center

wrap center

2 Sugarcoat

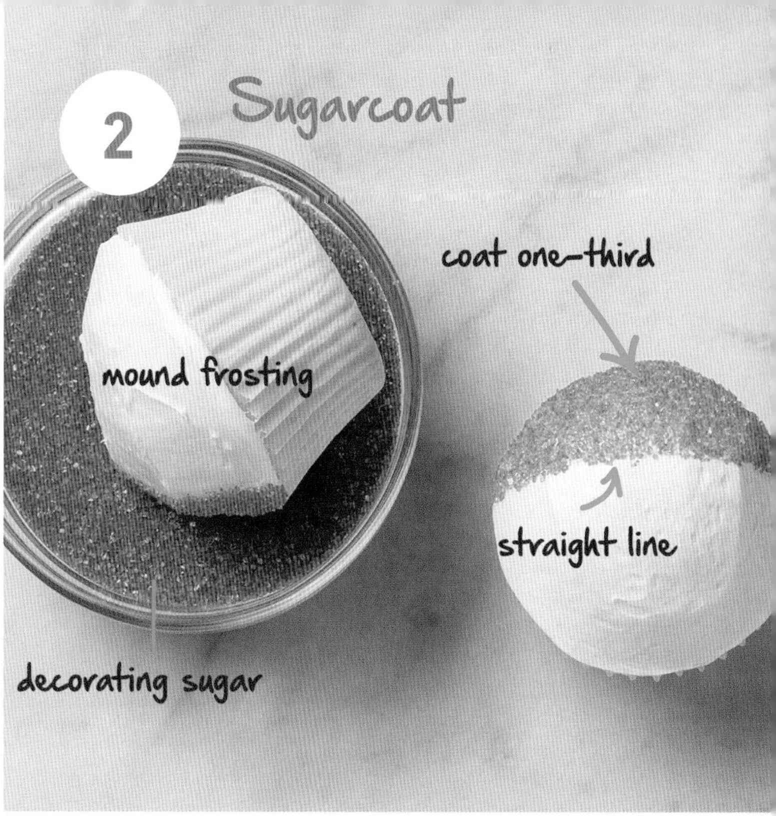

mound frosting

decorating sugar

coat one-third

straight line

3 Decorate

insert pretzel

attach spice drop

frosting

add décors

4 Add handle & bow

cover hole with bow

push straw into cupcake

insert stick in straw

81

Bows Art!

Flat candy, rolled-out candy, and gum in sticks, strips, or tape can be looped or pinched to make decorative bows.

use a large dot of frosting in the center to attach loops

start with outside row of loops

use fresh gum & work quickly so it stays flexible

add more loops to center

fold gum into loops

Hubba Bubble Bubble Tape

pinch ends

notch tail pieces

sour belt

Welch's fruit roll

pinch center and wrap
with small strip

Joray fruit
leather roll

Fruit by the Foot

sour
belt

Laffy Taffy

Hubba Bubba Bubble Tape

stick bubble gum

WE BAKED A ZOO

Critter cupcakes as easy as 1-2-3-ROAR!

FIDO'S SPOTS

mini M&M

large gumdrop

red frosting

vanilla wafer

red spray food coloring

red Dot gumdrop

Margherite cookie

mini M&M

green sprinkles

vanilla wafer

Oreo cookie

frosting

pink fruit chew

black pearls

red jelly bean

FIRE HYDRANTS

12 vanilla cupcakes, chilled
6 vanilla Margherite cookies, such as Stella D'oro
12 vanilla wafers
1 (16-ounce) can vanilla frosting
Red and neon blue food coloring, such as McCormick
1 (1.5-ounce) can red decorating spray, such as Cake Mate
6 large red gumdrops
12 red Dots gumdrops
½ cup green sprinkles
48 red M&M's Minis

1. Use a small serrated knife to saw ¼ inch from each short end of the Margherite cookies and then saw each cookie in half crosswise. Saw the vanilla wafers in half.

2. Put ¼ cup of the frosting in a bowl and tint it red with the food coloring. Spoon the tinted frosting into a zip-top bag and snip a small corner from the bag. Use a dot of red frosting to attach the flat side of a wafer half to one end of each Margherite cookie, and the curved side of another wafer half to the opposite end, and place on a sheet of waxed paper. Spray the assemblies with the red decorating spray to coat and let dry. Once dry, spray the hydrants again to intensify the color; let dry.

3. For the hydrant bonnet and outlets, place the large gumdrops, flat-side down, and cut them in half. Place the Dots on their side and trim ⅛ inch from the flat end. Position the larger piece cut-side down and cut in half.

4. Tint the remaining frosting pale blue with the food coloring. Spread some of the blue frosting on top of the cupcakes and smooth. For the grass, put the green sprinkles into a bowl and dip one edge of each cupcake about ½ inch into the sprinkles. Arrange a cookie hydrant on each cupcake above the grass. Using dots of red frosting, attach a gumdrop bonnet to the top end of each cookie hydrant, a flat Dot piece to the front, and a half Dot piece to each side. Use frosting to attach mini M&M's to the gumdrops and Dot pieces, and pipe a decorative line at the base of the gumdrops.

Makes 12 cupcakes

1 Cut cookies

trim ends

hydrant assembly

vanilla wafer

Margherite cookie

cut in half

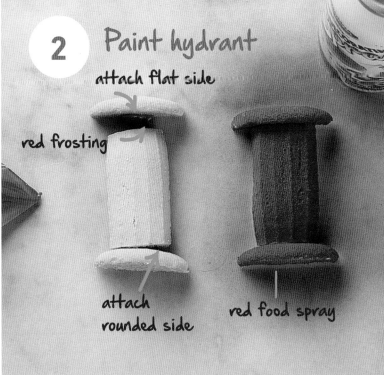

2 Paint hydrant

attach flat side

red frosting

attach rounded side

red food spray

3 Cut bonnet & outlets

trim bottoms of Dots

flat piece

half piece

cut gumdrop in half

split Dots in half

4 Assemble hydrant

frosting

mini M&M

sprinkles grass

half piece

89

BARKING DOGS

12 vanilla cupcakes, chilled
18 Oreos
1 (16-ounce) can vanilla frosting
3 pink Laffy Taffy
24 black pearls, such as SweetWorks
12 red jelly beans

1. Use a small serrated knife to saw 6 Oreos in half. Separate the Oreo halves—remove and discard the creme—to make 24 cookie ears. Saw ¼ inch from the remaining whole Oreos, discarding the small trimmings, to make 12 cookie muzzles.

2. Divide the frosting between two zip-top bags (it's easier to handle in two smaller bags than in one large one). Snip a small corner from the bags. Use a dot of frosting to attach a muzzle to the lower third of each cupcake, cut edge facing out. Use frosting to attach 2 ears to the top edge of the cupcakes, cut sides facing the same direction.

3. For the fur, pipe spikes of frosting, always pulling away from the center of the cupcake, starting along the outside edge of the cupcakes. Pipe lines along the rounded edge of the ears.

4. Continue to pipe frosting in overlapping rows to cover the cupcakes. Pipe short lines of frosting over the top edge of the muzzles and add a row of dots along the bottom, leaving the mouth area of the cookies exposed. For the tongue, cut the pink fruit chews into quarters and form each piece into a teardrop shape. Use a knife to make a line down the center. Press a tongue into the frosting at the bottom of the mouth. Add black pearls for the eyes and a red jelly bean for the nose.

Makes 12 cupcakes

1 Cut ears & muzzle

remove creme from ears

keep creme in muzzle

discard small piece

2 Attach parts

ears

frosting

muzzle

3 Pipe fur

pipe outside edge first

squeeze & pull to pipe spikes

4 Make dog face

pearl eyes

cover with fur

jelly bean nose

leave mouth exposed

fruit chew

shape tongue

91

HOW THE COOKIE CRUMBLES . . .

peanut butter wafer

chocolate wafer

strawberry wafer

vanilla wafer

frosting

wafer crumbs

sugar wafers

mega M&M's

NECCO wafers

M&M

mini marshmallows

dark chocolate frosting

LUCKY KITTY

12 vanilla cupcakes, chilled
1 (14.1-ounce) package sugar wafers, any
  flavor
1 (16-ounce) can vanilla frosting
¼ cup dark chocolate frosting
24 thin pretzel sticks
6 pink NECCO wafers
24 green NECCO wafers
24 brown M&M's Mega
12 red M&M's
12 mini marshmallows

1. For the ears, trim 1 inch from one end of 12 wafers. Cut the 1-inch piece on an angle to make 24 small triangles. For the paws, round one short end of the 12 larger pieces and trim ½ inch from the opposite end; save the trimmings. For the fur, put the remaining cookies along with the trimmings in a food processor and pulse into fine crumbs. Put the crumbs in a bowl.
2. Spoon ¼ cup of the vanilla frosting into a zip-top bag and the dark chocolate frosting into a separate bag. Spread a mound of the remaining vanilla frosting on top of each cupcake and smooth. Roll the tops of the cupcakes in the cookie crumbs to coat. Gently pat to reshape.
3. Snip a very small corner from the bags of frosting. Use some vanilla frosting to attach the ear cookies at the top edge of the cupcake. Insert 2 pretzel sticks horizontally into the right edge of each cupcake level with the liner, leaving ¾ inch exposed to support the paw. Cut the pink NECCO wafers in half. Use dots of vanilla frosting to secure one pink half NECCO on the lower half of each cupcake, cut side toward the center, for the mouth, and 2 green NECCOs on the upper half of the cupcakes for the eyes.
4. For the nose, push the side of a red M&M into the frosting, horizontally, just above the mouth. Using the chocolate frosting, pipe whiskers on the face and claws on each paw. For the cheeks, snip the mini marshmallows in half crosswise. Attach 2 marshmallow halves side by side, sticky-side down, on the pink NECCO mouth. Pipe 3 dots of dark chocolate frosting on each marshmallow. For the eyes, pipe a dot of vanilla frosting in the center of each green Necco and attach a mega M&M. Pipe a pair of white dot reflections, one large and one small, on each mega M&M. Pipe a line of frosting on the pretzel supports and place a wafer paw on top. Outline the paws and the ears with vanilla frosting.

Makes 12 cupcakes

1 Make paws & ears

round end
paw
1-inch square
diagonal cut
ears
ground cookies

2 Crumb coat

mound frosting
ground cookies
pink fur

3 Build face

wafer ear
frosting
NECCO eyes & mouth
pretzel support

4 Finish features

vanilla frosting
chocolate frosting
mega M&M eye
M&M nose
mini marshmallow cheek

95

HOW NOW, BROWN COW?

banana Runts

mini Oreos

sprinkles

Vienna Fingers

Sixlets

Nutter Butter

chocolate frosting with vanilla spots

Laffy Taffy

Froot Loops

Lotus Biscoff cookies

A Cow of an Udderly Different Color!

vanilla frosting with chocolate spots

chocolate E.L. Fudge Elfwich

potato sticks

CHOCOLATE COWS

12 chocolate cupcakes, chilled
1 (16-ounce) can chocolate frosting
½ cup vanilla frosting
9 Vienna Fingers, or similar-shaped
  cookies
3 Oreo Minis
2 pink Laffy Taffy
24 banana Runts
24 black Sixlets
Chocolate sprinkles
24 pink Froot Loops

1. Spread the top of the cupcakes with chocolate frosting and smooth. Put them on a cookie sheet and freeze for 15 minutes. Spoon ¼ cup of the vanilla frosting into each of two separate zip-top bags. Microwave one bag for 3 seconds, massaging the frosting to soften. Snip a small corner from the bag and pipe random frosting spots on top of the chilled cupcakes.

2. Separate the Vienna Fingers—remove and discard the creme—to make 18 cookies. For the chins, use a small serrated knife to saw 1 inch from each end of 6 of the cookies, discarding the center. (Reserve the 12 remaining uncut cookies for the muzzles.)

3. For the ears, separate the mini Oreos—remove and discard the creme—to make 6 cookies. Saw the mini cookies in half with a small serrated knife. For the tongues, cut the fruit chews into 12 small pieces and shape into small,

Vienna Fingers

E.L. Fudge Elfwich

Nutter Butter

Social Tea biscuit

Milano

Lotus Biscoff cookie

Hannover Waffeln

The Right Cookie Could Be Right Under Your Nose!

½-inch semicircles. Use a knife to score a line down the center of each.

4. Snip a small corner from the remaining bag of vanilla frosting. Use a dot of frosting to attach a muzzle cookie on the lower half of the cupcakes. Press the chin cookie into the frosting under the muzzle. For the horns, insert 2 banana candies, curved-side out, near the top edge of the cupcakes. Press the Oreo ears into the frosting on either side of the horns, curved-side up. Pipe frosting dots for the eyes and add a Sixlet to each. Insert 3 chocolate sprinkles as eyelashes above each eye. Use frosting to attach the cereal nostrils to the muzzles, and the fruit chew tongue to the chins.

Makes 12 cupcakes

VARIATION:

Frost the cupcakes with vanilla frosting and use softened chocolate frosting for the spots. Replace the Vienna Fingers cookies with chocolate E.L.Fudge Elfwiches.

1 Pipe spots

softened vanilla frosting

chilled chocolate frosting

2 Create muzzle

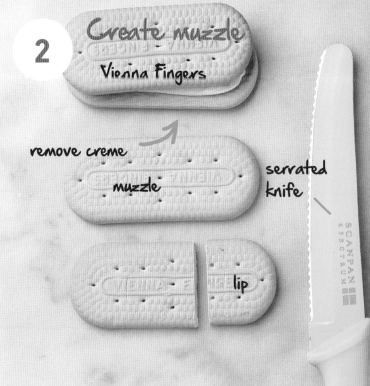

Vienna Fingers

remove creme

muzzle

serrated knife

lip

SCANPAN SPECTRUM

3 Cut ears & tongue

mini Oreos

remove creme

Laffy Taffy

ears

tongues

4 Make faces

banana Runt horns

frosting

sprinkles

tongue

Froot Loops

Sixlets

99

LET'S BE SHELLFISH!

dark chocolate frosting

mini marshmallows

pretzel sticks

Fruit by the Foot

mini doughnut

red licorice laces

red gumdrops

vanilla cookie crumbs

madeleine cookies

pink frosting

green apple twists

mini gumball

blue frosting

madeleine cookie crumbs

CRABBY CRAB CUPCAKES

12 vanilla cupcakes, chilled

12 mini marshmallows

1 (10-ounce) bag red melting wafers, such as Wilton

12 mini powdered doughnuts, such as Entenmann's

2 tablespoons red decorating sugar, such as Cake Mate

24 thin pretzel sticks

12 large red gumdrops

1 (16-ounce) can vanilla frosting

½ cup ground vanilla wafers, about 10

9 strands red licorice lace, such as Twizzlers Pull'n'Peel

1 (.75-ounce) roll strawberry fruit leather, such as Fruit by the Foot

¼ cup dark chocolate frosting

1. Snip the mini marshmallows in half crosswise; set aside. Put the red melting wafers in a small bowl and microwave in 5-second increments, stirring after each, until smooth. Line a cookie sheet with waxed paper. Brush any excess sugar from the doughnuts and dip two-thirds of the doughnut into the melted candy, allowing the excess to drip back into the bowl. Transfer to the lined cookie sheet and while still wet sprinkle with some red sugar. Hold the pretzel sticks by an end and dip into the melted candy up to your fingers, allow the excess to drip back into the bowl. Transfer to the waxed paper and, while still wet, attach the flat side of a cut marshmallow to the coated tip of each pretzel. Refrigerate until set.

2. For the claws, place a gumdrop flat-side down and cut it in half. Place each half cut-side down and remove a ¼-inch wedge from one round end, reserving the pieces.

3. For the body, make a straight cut in the doughnuts to remove and discard the uncoated portion. Use a toothpick to make 2 holes, about 1 inch apart, on the top edge of the doughnuts. Trim the uncoated end from the pretzel sticks and insert one into each hole.

4. For the legs, cut the licorice laces into seventy-two 1-inch pieces. For the mouths, cut the fruit leather into twelve 1¼-inch pieces, fold each piece in half lengthwise, and press together. Starting at a short end, make small folds back and forth like folding a fan. Pinch the fan at the bottom and open the opposite end. To assemble the crabs, spread some vanilla frosting on top of the cupcakes and smooth. Sprinkle with the cookie crumbs as sand. Press a doughnut, cut-side down, into the frosting on one side of each cupcake. Attach 3 licorice legs on either side of the doughnuts. Arrange 2 cut gumdrops and 2 small reserved gumdrop pieces as the claws on each cupcake. Use a dot of melted red candy to attach a fruit leather mouth to the top of the doughnuts. Put the dark chocolate frosting in a zip-top bag. Snip a small corner from the bag. Pipe dark chocolate frosting eyes on the marshmallows.

Makes 12 cupcakes

1 Candycoat shell

melted candy

decorating sugar

pretzel stick

mini marshmallow

dip & sprinkle sugar

mini doughnut

2 Create claws

large gumdrop

claw

arm joint

3 Carve shell

toothpick

insert pretzel

make hole

snap off end

trim doughnut

4 Assemble

cookie crumbs

licorice legs

gather & pinch fruit leather mouth

OYSTERS WITH PEARLS

12 vanilla cupcakes, chilled
3 green apple licorice twists, such as Kenny's Candy Juicy Twists
24 madeleine cookies, such as Entenmann's
1 (16-ounce) can vanilla frosting
Neon pink and neon blue food coloring, such as McCormick
12 small pearlized gumballs, such as SweetWorks

1. Cut the green licorice twists into 1-inch pieces. Cut each piece lengthwise on an angle to make tapered blades of seagrass.
2. Use a small serrated knife to saw the hump from the top side of the madeleines. Crumble the scraps into fine crumbs to use as sand.
3. Put ⅔ cup of the frosting in a bowl and tint it light pink with the food coloring. Spoon the frosting into a zip-top bag. Tint the remaining frosting light blue with the food coloring. Spread some of the blue frosting on top of each cupcake and smooth. Add a trimmed cookie, scallop-side down, to the top of each cupcake. Sprinkle some of the cookie sand on the blue frosting.
4. Snip a ¼-inch corner from the bag with the pink frosting. Pipe a zigzag of pink frosting on top of the cookie on the cupcakes as the oysters. Add a gumball to one side as the pearl. Top with the remaining cookie, scallop-side up, leaving the pearl slightly exposed. Insert 2 or 3 blades of licorice seagrass next to each oyster.

Makes 12 cupcakes

1 Cut the grass

green apple twists

diagonal cut

FISKARS

tapered ends

2 Trim the shells

madeleine cookie

crumble hump for sand

remove hump

BRANDANI INOX

3 Add shell & sand

scallop-side down

cookie crumb sand

blue frosting

4 Stuff the oyster

pink frosting

zigzag shape

gumball pearl

seagrass

scallop-side up

105

CHEW ON THIS!

BUSY BEAVERS

12 chocolate cupcakes, chilled
1 (16-ounce) can chocolate frosting
6 marshmallows
24 brown M&M's
24 black Sixlets
12 black gumdrops, such as Crows
12 mini marshmallows
12 butter waffle cookies, such as Jules Destrooper Butter Crisps
Rolled wafer cookies, such as Pepperidge Farm

butter waffle cookie

chocolate frosting

mini marshmallow

rolled wafer cookie

1. Working on one cupcake at a time to prevent the frosting from drying, spread a mound of chocolate frosting on top and smooth. For the muzzle, snip the marshmallows in half crosswise. Place one half on top of the cupcake, sticky-side down. Use more frosting to cover the marshmallow and smooth.
2. To create the fur, use a fork to lightly pull the frosting along the outer edge, away from the center, wiping the fork clean every two or three strokes. For the ears, insert 2 M&M's upright in the pulled frosting edge, about 2 inches apart.
3. Continue to pull the frosting, always away from the center, in concentric overlapping circles, to cover the cupcake and marshmallow nose.
4. For the eyes, add 2 Sixlets about 1 inch in from the ears. For the nose, add a black gumdrop on its side, with the flat edge up, at the center of the cupcake. For the teeth, snip a mini marshmallow in half lengthwise and add it below the nose. Place a waffle cookie at the base of the cupcake for the tail. Break some of the rolled wafer cookies into 2-inch pieces and add to the plate for logs. Repeat with the remaining cupcakes.

Makes 12 cupcakes

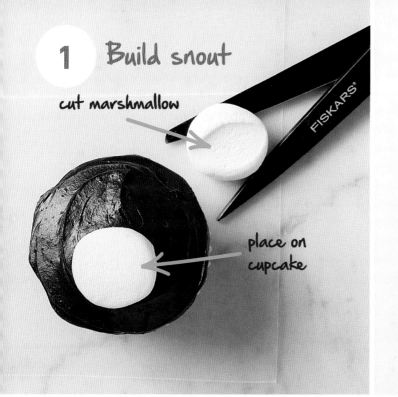

1 Build snout

cut marshmallow

place on cupcake

2 Start forking

upright M&M ears

forked edge

frost marshmallow

3 Fur coat

pull away from center

overlap rows

keep fork clean

4 Add features

Sixlets eyes

black gumdrop nose

waffle cookie tail

mini marshmallow teeth

BUCKY THE CHIPMUNK

12 spice cupcakes, chilled
18 mini marshmallows
2 tablespoons pink decorating sugar, such as Cake Mate
6 pink NECCO wafers
½ cup vanilla frosting
1 (16-ounce) can salted caramel frosting
6 Nutter Butter cookies
24 brown M&M's Minis
12 pink jelly beans

1. For the ears, snip 12 of the mini marshmallows in half on an angle. Put the decorating sugar in a small bowl and dip the sticky sides of the marshmallows in the sugar to coat.
2. For the mouth, use a small serrated knife to score the NECCO wafers in half; snap each wafer in two along the scored line. For the teeth, snip the remaining 6 mini marshmallows end to end, and then snip each piece end to end again, to make 24 teeth.
3. Spoon the vanilla frosting into a zip-top bag and ½ cup of the caramel frosting into a separate bag. Spread the remaining caramel frosting on top of the cupcakes and smooth. For the cheeks, separate the Nutter Butters—remove and discard the filling—to make 12 cookies. Place one cookie on the lower third of each cupcake, flat-side down, as the cheeks. Add the marshmallow ears at the top edge, sugared-side facing up, about 1 inch apart. Snip a small corner from the bags of frosting. Use caramel frosting to outline each ear. Starting at the cookie edge, pipe 2 lines of vanilla frosting between the ears to make a stripe. For the eyes, add dots of vanilla frosting on either side of the stripe.
4. Add mini M&M's to the eyes. Use dots of frosting to attach the jelly bean nose above the cookie, a NECCO Wafer mouth to the center of the cookie, and mini marshmallow teeth to the mouth.

Makes 12 cupcakes

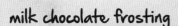
milk chocolate frosting

Nutter Butter cookie

salted caramel frosting

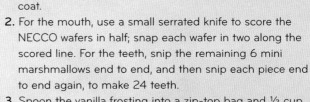

VARIATION:

Make chocolate chipmunks by using milk chocolate frosting in place of salted caramel.

1 Make ears

mini marshmallow

diagonal cut

decorating sugar

2 Make buck teeth

mini marshmallow

NECCO wafer

cut once

score

cut again

snap

mouth & teeth

3 Pipe fur

frosting

caramel frosting

cookie cheeks

remove & discard filling

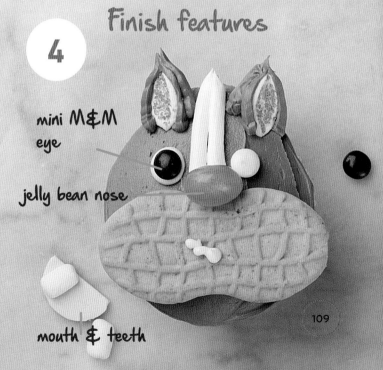

4 Finish features

mini M&M eye

jelly bean nose

mouth & teeth

109

WHITE LAB MICE

12 vanilla cupcakes, chilled
1 (16-ounce) can vanilla frosting
36 mini vanilla wafers, such as Nilla Wafers
2 cups desiccated coconut
12 small pink jelly beans, such as Jelly Belly
24 black pearls, such as SweetWorks
4 black licorice laces

1. Spoon ½ cup of vanilla frosting into a zip-top bag. Spread the top of the cupcakes with a mound of the remaining frosting and smooth. For the heads, place a vanilla wafer on each cupcake, flat-side down, overhanging the edge slightly. For the ears, add 2 more wafers against the back of the head, standing up with the flat side facing out.
2. Snip a small corner from the bag of frosting. Pipe some frosting over the cookie head to cover. Pipe a line of frosting around the cookie ears.

3. Sprinkle the coconut over the cupcakes, making sure to cover the tops completely. Remove any excess coconut from the frosted areas and use a small brush to expose the unfrosted center of the ears. Gently press the coconut to reshape.
4. Pipe a dot of frosting on the front tip of each head and add a jelly bean nose. Add the pearl eyes, pressing them into the frosting to secure. For the tail, cut the licorice lace into twelve 3-inch pieces. Insert a tail in the frosting on the edge of the cupcakes, opposite the head.

Makes 12 cupcakes

VARIATION:

You can make the mice any color; simply tint the desiccated coconut with food coloring and spread it on waxed paper to dry before using.

licorice lace

mini vanilla wafer

black pearl

jelly bean

coconut

1 Add head & ears

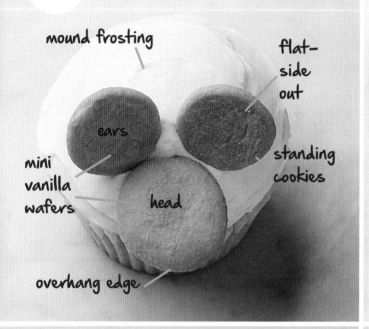

mound frosting

ears

flat-side out

mini vanilla wafers

standing cookies

head

overhang edge

2 Pipe frosting

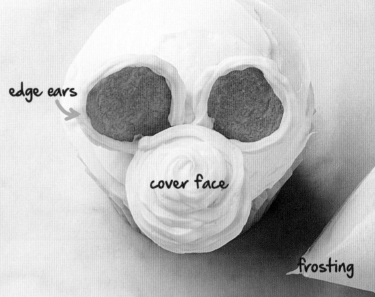

edge ears

cover face

frosting

3 Fur coat

press to smooth

brush coconut from unfrosted area

desiccated coconut

4 Add face & tail

pearl eyes

licorice lace tail

jelly bean nose

frosting

CHEESE SLICE

12 vanilla cupcakes, chilled
12 circus peanuts
1 (16-ounce) can vanilla frosting
Yellow food coloring, such as McCormick

1. Place the circus peanuts on their side and cut them lengthwise into thirds.
2. Arrange 3 slices flat-side down and slightly overlapping. Roll the slices, pressing them together into roughly 2¼-inch shapes.
3. Trim the rolled candy into 2-inch squares. For the holes, use pastry tips, straws, or a cookie cutter to remove small holes of various sizes from each square.
4. Tint the vanilla frosting pale yellow. Spread the frosting on top of the cupcakes and smooth. Place a cheese slice on top of each cupcake.

Makes 12 cupcakes

Grey Lab Mice, variation page 110

112

1 Process cheese

circus peanut

place on side

make 3 slices

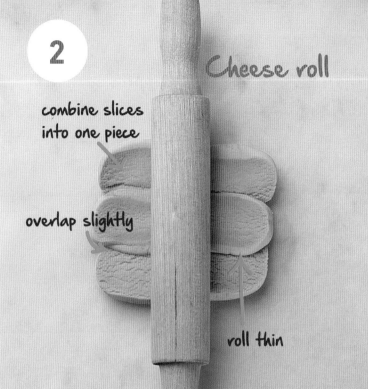

2 Cheese roll

combine slices into one piece

overlap slightly

roll thin

3 Cut the cheese

square slice

pastry tip

big & small holes

straws

4 Serve cheese

yellow frosting

SAFARI, SO GOOD

mini M&M's

Pringles

pearl decorating spray

decorating sugar

banana Runts

jumbo marshmallow

pretzels

sprinkles

mini vanilla wafers

Apple Jacks

jelly bean

mini marshmallows

fruit leather

circus peanuts

vanilla wafer

heart Runts

JUNGLE BOOGIE

Oreos

M&M's

mini M&M's

decorating sugar

mini marshmallows

jelly beans

mini M&M's

NECCO wafers

Oreo

mini M&M

circus peanut

mini Oreo

Nitwitz Kooky Bananas

Oreo

ELEPHANTS

12 vanilla cupcakes, chilled
3 jumbo marshmallows, such as Campfire
12 Pringles potato chips
1 (1.5-ounce) can pink or pearl decorating spray, such as Wilton
1 (16-ounce) can vanilla frosting
1 cup pink or white pearl decorating sugar, such as Wilton
24 brown M&M's Minis
24 banana Runts

1. For the trunks, cut the jumbo marshmallows in half through the rounded side, on a slight angle. Snip each piece in half from thin to thick end. Trim the wide end of each resulting piece to even the top of the trunk. Transfer the pieces to a sheet of waxed paper, spacing them about 1 inch apart.
2. For the ears, snap the Pringles in half on an angle. Arrange them on the sheet of waxed paper in pairs, rounded edges out away from each other, about 1 inch apart. Spray all the pieces with one color of decorating spray to coat and let dry. Once dry, spray again to intensify the color; let dry.
3. Spoon ½ cup of the vanilla frosting into a zip-top bag. Snip a small corner from the bag. Pipe 4 or 5 evenly spaced lines across the curved side of the trunk. Put the decorating sugar that matches the spray color in a bowl and sprinkle the lines with the sugar. Spread a mound of the remaining frosting on top of each cupcake and smooth. Roll the tops of the cupcakes in the sugar to coat. Gently pat to reshape.
4. Pipe some frosting on the lower third of the cupcakes and attach a marshmallow trunk with the narrow end extending over the cupcake edge. Pipe 2 dots of frosting above the trunk for the eyes and add the mini M&M's. Insert the rounded ends of the paired Pringles ears into the frosting on either side of the cupcakes. Insert the banana candy tusks on either side of the trunks.

Makes 12 cupcakes

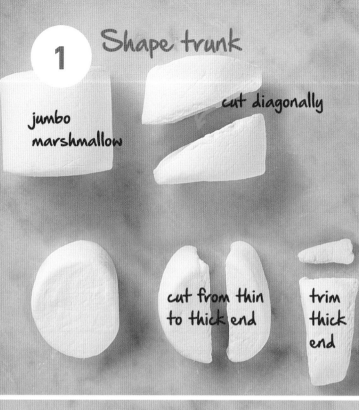

1 Shape trunk

jumbo marshmallow

cut diagonally

cut from thin to thick end

trim thick end

2 Spray parts

Pringles

snap on diagonal

decorating spray

ears

marshmallow trunk

3 Sugarcoat

decorating sugar

mound frosting

pipe lines & sprinkle

4 Assemble

frosting

banana Runt tusks

mini M&M eyes

117

1. Use a small serrated knife to saw the pretzel sticks and the mini vanilla wafers in half.
2. Spoon the caramel frosting, the dark chocolate frosting, and ¼ cup of the vanilla frosting into separate zip-top bags. Spread some of the remaining vanilla frosting on top of each cupcake and smooth. Snip a small corner from the bags of frosting. Pipe small irregular spots (¼ to ½ inch) of caramel frosting on top of the cupcakes. Put the decorating sugar in a bowl and roll the tops of the cupcakes in the sugar to coat. Gently pat to reshape.
3. For the muzzle, pipe a dot of vanilla frosting near one edge of each cupcake and attach the whole vanilla wafer, flat-side down, hanging slightly over the edge. For the horns, insert the cut end of 2 pretzel pieces opposite the muzzle, about 1 inch apart, leaving ¾ inch of the pretzel exposed. Press the vanilla wafer ears into the frosting on either side of the horns, curved side toward horns.
4. Pipe dots of vanilla frosting for the eyes and add the mini M&M's. Add the chocolate sprinkles for the eyelashes. Pipe dots of dark chocolate frosting on top of the vanilla wafers for nostrils. Use a dot of vanilla frosting to add a candy heart under the edge of the vanilla wafer as a mouth.

Makes 12 cupcakes

FUN IDEA:
Make additional cupcakes through step 2 and arrange them in a diagonal line to look like a long giraffe neck.

GIRAFFES

12 vanilla cupcakes, chilled
12 pretzel dipping sticks, such as Snyder's of Hanover
12 mini vanilla wafers, such as Nilla Wafers
1 cup caramel frosting
¼ cup dark chocolate frosting
1 (16-ounce) can vanilla frosting
1 cup yellow decorating sugar, such as Cake Mate
12 vanilla wafers
24 brown M&M's Minis
1 tablespoon chocolate sprinkles
12 red heart Runts

1 Cut horns & ears

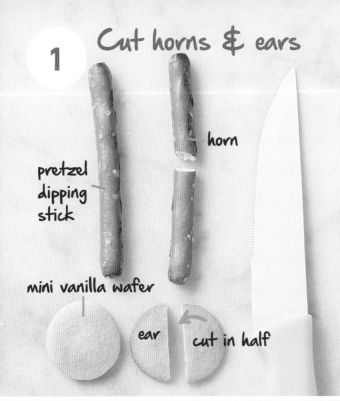

horn

pretzel
dipping
stick

mini vanilla wafer

ear

cut in half

2 Sugarcoat spots

irregular spots

caramel
frosting

yellow
decorating
sugar

3 Attach parts

insert horns

insert ears

secure
with
frosting

vanilla
wafer
nose

4 Add features

frosting

mini
M&M
eyes

sprinkles
lashes

dark chocolate
frosting

heart Runt
tongue

LIONS

12 vanilla cupcakes, chilled
27 circus peanuts
12 mini marshmallows
4 inches strawberry fruit leather, such as Fruit by the Foot
1 (16-ounce) can vanilla frosting
Red and yellow food coloring, such as McCormick
¼ cup dark chocolate frosting
12 small brown jelly beans, such as Jelly Belly
24 orange Apple Jacks cereal pieces

1. Place the circus peanuts on their side and cut them in half lengthwise to make 54 pieces. Flatten the slices with a rolling pin to make 1¼ by 2½-inch pieces.
2. For the mane, cut 48 of the rolled slices in half crosswise, and the remaining 6 rolled slices in quarters. Snip small notches from the curved ends of each piece, making 4 points on the 96 large pieces and 3 points on the 24 small pieces. Taper the sides slightly to the flat end. For the cheeks, snip the mini marshmallows in half crosswise. For the tongue, cut the fruit leather into twelve ½-inch teardrop shapes.
3. Tint the vanilla frosting orange with the red and yellow food coloring. Spread a mound of the frosting on top of each cupcake and smooth. For each cupcake, position 4 large mane pieces, one at each corner, with the pointed ends overhanging the edge. Press 4 more large mane pieces into the frosting, in between and overlapping the corner pieces. For the beard under the chin, attach 2 small mane pieces at the bottom, about ½ inch apart.
4. Spoon the dark chocolate frosting into a zip-top bag. Add a jelly bean, horizontally, to the center of each cupcake as the nose. Arrange 2 marshmallow cheeks below the nose, cut-side down. Snip a very small corner from the bag of frosting. Pipe 3 frosting dots on the cheeks and add a dot for each eye. Add the Apple Jack cereal ears. Press the fruit leather tongue into the frosting below the cheeks.

Makes 12 cupcakes

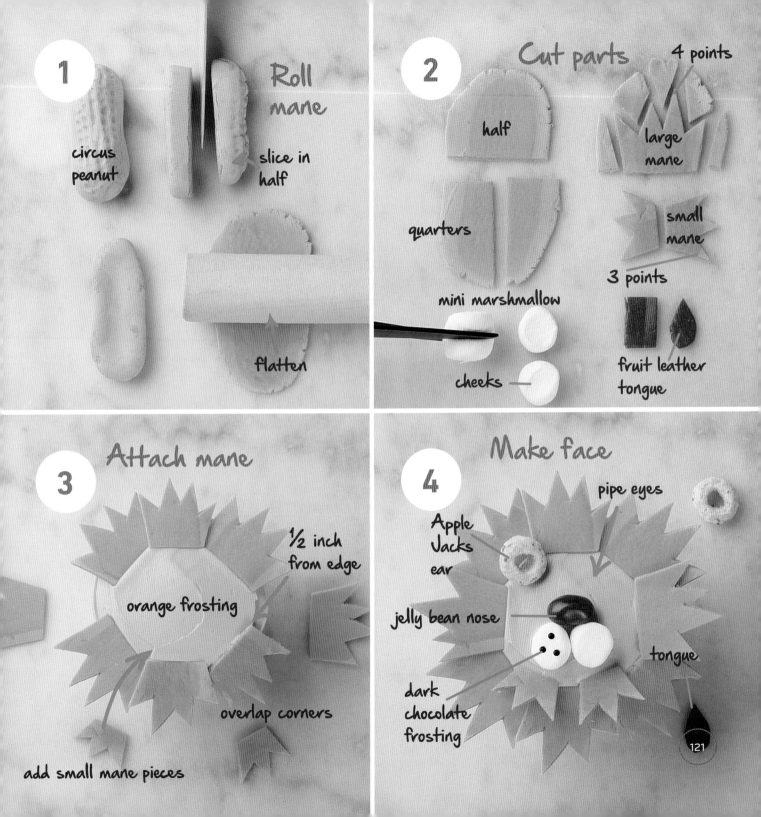

1 Roll mane

circus peanut

slice in half

flatten

2 Cut parts

half

4 points

large mane

quarters

small mane

3 points

mini marshmallow

cheeks

fruit leather tongue

3 Attach mane

½ inch from edge

orange frosting

overlap corners

add small mane pieces

4 Make face

pipe eyes

Apple Jacks ear

jelly bean nose

tongue

dark chocolate frosting

121

GORILLAS

12 chocolate cupcakes, chilled
12 Oreos
1 (16-ounce) can chocolate frosting
¼ cup vanilla frosting
1 cup black decorating sugar, such as Wilton
24 brown M&M's Minis
24 brown M&M's

1. Separate the Oreos—remove and discard the creme—to make 24 cookies. Use a small serrated knife to saw 12 of the cookies in half for the heads and brows. With the remaining 12 cookies, saw off one-third of the cookie for the lip and use the remaining two-thirds for the chin.
2. Spoon ¼ cup of the chocolate frosting into a zip-top bag and the vanilla frosting into a separate bag.

Spread a mound of the remaining chocolate frosting on top of each cupcake and smooth. Put the decorating sugar in a bowl and roll the cupcake edge in the sugar to coat by about ¾ inch. Gently pat to reshape.
3. Press a half cookie into the frosting at the top of the cupcake for the head and a two-thirds cookie at the bottom for the chin, allowing the rounded sides of the cookies to overhang the edge by ½ inch. Snip a small corner from the bag of vanilla frosting. Pipe dots of vanilla frosting ½ inch apart just above the center of the cupcake for the eyes.
4. Add the mini M&M's to the dots of vanilla frosting. Insert the half cookie brow at the edge of the head cookie, cut-side down and angled over the eyes. For the lip, snip a small corner from the bag of chocolate frosting and use a dot of chocolate frosting to attach the one-third cookie to the top of the chin, curved-side up. Pipe chocolate nostrils on the lip cookie. Add the M&M ears on either side of the head.

Makes 12 cupcakes

1 Cut forehead & mouth

remove creme

Oreo

crown

brow

cut in half

lip

chin

cut one third

2 Sugarcoat edge

black decorating sugar

mound chocolate frosting

roll edge

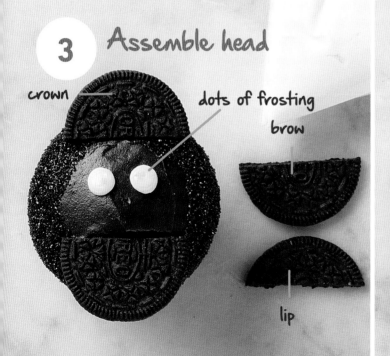

3 Assemble head

crown

dots of frosting

brow

lip

4 Attach features

chocolate frosting

mini M&M eye

M&M ear

pipe nostrils

TIGERS

12 vanilla cupcakes, chilled
4 Oreos
36 mini marshmallows
1 cup orange decorating sugar, such as Wilton
½ cup dark chocolate frosting
1 (16-ounce) can vanilla frosting
24 orange NECCO wafers
12 small brown jelly beans, such as Jelly Belly
24 brown M&M's Minis

1. Separate the Oreos—remove and discard the creme—to make 8 cookies. Use a small serrated knife to saw the cookies in half.
2. Snip the mini marshmallows in half on an angle. For the ears, put the decorating sugar in a bowl and dip 24 marshmallow halves in the sugar to coat. Leave the remaining marshmallow halves plain for the fur.
3. Spoon the dark chocolate frosting into a zip-top bag and ¼ cup of the vanilla frosting into a separate bag. Snip a very small corner from the bags. Spread a mound of the remaining vanilla frosting on top of each cupcake and smooth. Pipe 8 evenly spaced zigzag lines of the dark chocolate frosting on top of each cupcake, starting wider at the edge of the cupcake and narrow at the center. Roll the tops in the orange sugar to coat. Gently pat to reshape.
4. To assemble, use the dark chocolate frosting to attach an Oreo half, cut side to the center, on the lower half of each cupcake. Pipe dots of the frosting on the Oreo and attach the NECCO wafer cheeks side by side. Add a dot of the frosting above the cheeks and attach the jelly bean nose. Pipe lines of dark chocolate whiskers on the cheeks. Pipe dots of vanilla frosting and attach the marshmallow ears about 2 inches apart on the top edge of each cupcake. Use the frosting to attach marshmallow fur along the bottom edge of the cupcakes. Pipe 2 dots of the vanilla frosting above the nose and add the M&M eyes.

Makes 12 cupcakes

1 Cut mouth

remove creme

Oreo

cut in half

mouth

BRAN

2 Ears & fur

mini marshmallows

snip on diagonal

sugared for ears

decorating sugar

uncoated for fur

3 Stripe & sugarcoat

pipe lines wide at edge

narrow at center

dark chocolate frosting

orange decorating sugar

4 Attach features

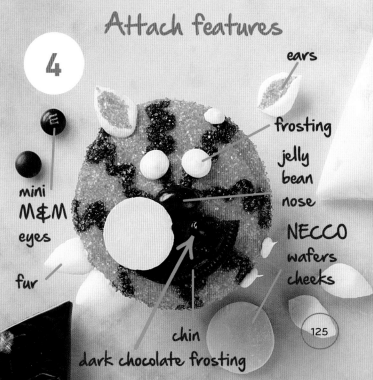

ears

frosting

jelly bean nose

NECCO wafers cheeks

mini M&M eyes

fur

chin
dark chocolate frosting

125

BEE EATERS

12 vanilla cupcakes, chilled
6 Oreos
12 Oreo Minis
4 circus peanuts
1 (16-ounce) can vanilla frosting
1 cup light green decorating sugar, such as Wilton
¼ cup dark chocolate frosting
84 Nitwitz Kooky Bananas
12 brown M&M's Minis

1. For the bodies, separate the large Oreos—remove and discard the creme—to make 12 cookies. Separate the mini Oreos, leaving the creme intact on one side. Set aside the 12 sides with creme for the eyes. Use a small serrated knife to saw 6 of the remaining mini cookies in half for the wings (there will be extra cookies for breakage).

2. For the beaks, cut the circus peanuts lengthwise into 3 slices. Make a curved cut ¼ inch from one short end of each slice to make the end concave.

3. Spoon the dark chocolate frosting into a zip-top bag and ¼ cup of the vanilla frosting into a separate bag. Frost the top of each cupcake with some of the remaining vanilla frosting and smooth. Put the decorating sugar in a bowl and roll the cupcake edge in the sugar to coat, leaving about 1 inch in the center uncoated. Gently pat to reshape.

4. For the bodies, press a large cookie into the frosting in the center of each cupcake, flat-side down. For the eyes, snip a very small corner from the bag of dark chocolate frosting and pipe a dot of the frosting on one edge of each body cookie and attach a mini Oreo cookie, cream-side up. Pipe a dot of dark chocolate frosting on the body cookie in front of each eye and attach a circus peanut beak, curved end against the eye cookie and straight-side down. Pipe another dot below each eye and add an Oreo wing, curved edge forward. Use the frosting to pipe a nostril on each beak near the head. For the feathers, insert 3 Kooky bananas into the frosting above the heads, and 4 more at the back of the bodies. Snip a very small corner from the bag of vanilla frosting. Pipe a dot of vanilla frosting on top of the eyes and add a mini M&M to the center of each.

Makes 12 cupcakes

1 Make body parts

Oreo

body

remove creme

mini Oreo

cut in half

eye, creme

wings, no creme

2 Trim beak

circus peanut

3 slices

concave end

discard

3 Sugarcoat edge

frosting

roll edge

decorating sugar

no sugar in center

4 Make bird

banana feathers

dots of frosting

mini M&M eye

place beak on cookie

mini Oreo wing

beak, straight-side down

127

NESSIE SIGHTING!

circus peanut

nonpareils

mini doughnut

blue frosting

mini M&M's

dark chocolate frosting

green candy coating

anisette
toast

LOCH NESS MONSTER

6 vanilla cupcakes, chilled

4 circus peanuts

4 mini cinnamon or plain doughnuts, such as Entenmann's

1 cup green or purple melting wafers, such as Wilton

2 anisette toasts, such as Stella D'oro

2 teaspoons orange nonpareils, such as Wilton

1 (16-ounce) can vanilla frosting

Neon blue food coloring, such as McCormick

2 tablespoons dark chocolate frosting

2 green or orange M&M's Minis

1. For the head, trim a small wedge, about ½ inch thick, from the flat side of a circus peanut. For the scales, cut the remaining circus peanuts in half lengthwise and roll them out thin. Cut each thin slice in half crosswise. Use pinking scissors to give each piece a sawtooth outer curve, about 1½ inches wide. Use plain scissors to give the opposite sides of 2 pieces a straight side for the back of the neck, and the remainder of the pieces a concave inner curve for the body. Make 12 scales.

2. Brush any excess sugar from the doughnuts. Line a cookie sheet with waxed paper. Put the melting wafers in a small bowl and microwave in 5-second increments, stirring after each, until smooth. Dip two-thirds of each doughnut into the melted candy. Allow the excess candy to drip back into the bowl. Transfer to the lined cookie sheet. Dip all but 1 inch of an anisette toast for the neck and dip half of the other toast for the tail, allowing the excess candy to drip back into the bowl. Transfer the pieces to the waxed paper, curved-side up. Sprinkle the coated parts with nonpareils while the candy is still wet. Attach the circus peanut head to the cookie neck, cut side pressed into the candy-coated tip (use an additional dot of wet candy if needed). Refrigerate until set, about 10 minutes.

3. Use a small serrated knife to saw the tail cookie and the dipped doughnuts in half, discarding the uncoated parts. (Do not trim the neck cookie.)

4. Tint the vanilla frosting pale blue with the food coloring. Spread the blue frosting on top of the cupcakes to look like water. Insert the uncoated end of the neck into the center of a cupcake. Add the tail cookie and the coated doughnuts, cut-sides down, each to the center of a separate cupcake. Spread a dot of water along the bottom edge of the straight-sided neck scales and attach them to the back of the neck cookie. Use dots of water to add 1 or 2 curved scales to the outer edge of each doughnut curve and the tail. Spoon the dark chocolate frosting into a zip-top bag. Snip a small corner from the bag. Pipe dark chocolate dots on either side of the head and attach the mini M&M eyes. Pipe dots at the center of the M&M's for pupils and pipe nostrils at the front end of the head.

Makes 6 cupcakes

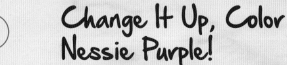

Change It Up, Color Nessie Purple!

1 Make head & scales

- circus peanut
- bevel one end for head
- cut in half for scales
- pinking scissors
- sawtooth curve
- roll thin

2 Coat parts

- melted candy
- mini doughnut
- attach head
- nonpareils
- wet candy

3 Trim parts

- cut in half
- discard uncoated portion

4 Assemble

- attach doughnut cut-side down
- push cookie in
- frosting
- mini M&M eyes
- water

131

GO WHOLE HOG!

mini Nutter Butter

Nutter Butter

small brown jelly beans

mini chocolate chips

frosting

small black jelly beans

Nutter Butter crumbs

chocolate frosting

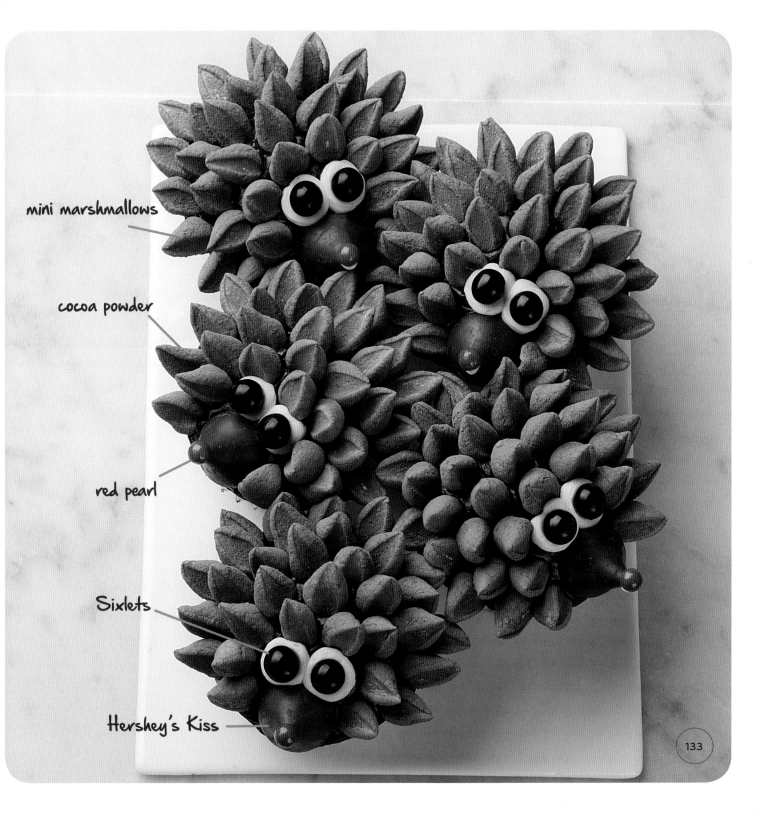

mini marshmallows

cocoa powder

red pearl

Sixlets

Hershey's Kiss

133

GROUNDHOGS

12 spice cupcakes, chilled
12 mini Nutter Butter cookies
1 cup light cocoa melting wafers, such as Wilton
14 Nutter Butter cookies
24 small brown jelly beans, such as Jelly Belly
12 small black jelly beans, such as Jelly Belly
¼ cup vanilla frosting
24 mini chocolate chips
1 (16-ounce) can chocolate frosting

1. Separate the mini Nutter Butters—remove and discard the filling—to make 24 cookies. Put the melting wafers in a zip-top bag and microwave in 5-second increments, massaging the bag after each, until smooth. Snip a small corner from the bag. Pipe 2 dots of melted candy side by side in the middle (narrow) area of 12 whole Nutter Butters and attach 2 of the mini cookies, flat-side down. Chill until set, about 5 minutes.

2. Using the melted candy, attach the brown jelly beans at the top edge of the Nutter Butter for ears. Attach the black jelly bean centered on top of the mini cookies for the nose. Spoon the vanilla frosting into a zip-top bag. Snip a small corner from the bag. For the eyes, pipe 2 dots of frosting above the nose and insert mini chips with their pointed end into the frosting. Pipe teeth below and between the mini cookie cheeks.

3. Spread a mound of chocolate frosting on top of each cupcake and smooth. Use a small knife to make a slit in the top of each cupcake.

4. Insert the bottom of a groundhog cookie into each slit. Crush the remaining 2 whole Nutter Butters into fine crumbs and sprinkle them around the base of the groundhogs as dirt.

Makes 12 cupcakes

Add a Cocoa Powder Shadow for Groundhog Day!

134

1 Attach cheeks

separate & remove filling

do not separate

Nutter Butter

melted candy

mini Nutter Butter

2 Add face

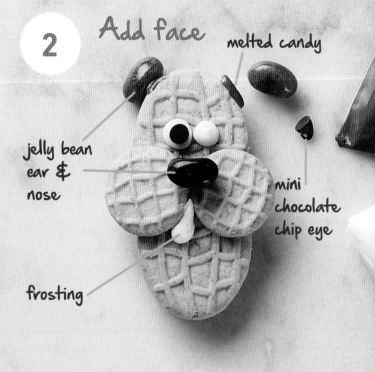

melted candy

jelly bean ear & nose

mini chocolate chip eye

frosting

3 Make slit

insert knife

4 Insert groundhog

push in

Nutter Butter crumbs

HEDGEHOGS

12 vanilla cupcakes, chilled
1 (10-ounce) bag mini marshmallows
½ cup unsweetened cocoa powder
1 (16-ounce) can chocolate frosting
12 chocolate Hershey's Kisses
¼ cup vanilla frosting
24 black Sixlets
12 red pearls, such as SweetWorks

1. Place the cocoa powder in a small container with
   a lid handy. Working in batches, snip the mini
   marshmallows in half on an angle and drop them into
   the container. Cover and shake until marshmallows
   are evenly coated. Remove the coated marshmallows,
   shaking the excess cocoa powder back into the
   container. Repeat to coat all of the marshmallows.

2. Working on one cupcake at a time to prevent the frosting
   from drying, spread the top with a mound of chocolate
   frosting and smooth. Place a chocolate Kiss, flat-side down,
   near one edge of the cupcake.

3. For the spines, press cocoa-coated marshmallows close
   together in rows, pointed ends up and curved sides facing
   the Kiss, to cover the top of the cupcake. Leave an opening
   in back of the Kiss for the eyes.

4. Spoon the vanilla frosting into a zip-top bag. Snip a small
   corner from the bag. Pipe 2 dots of frosting in the open
   space behind the Kiss. Add the Sixlets for eyes. Pipe a dot
   of frosting on the tip of the Kiss and add the pearl for a
   nose. Repeat with the remaining cupcakes.

Makes 12 cupcakes

1 Coat spines

shake in cocoa powder

mini marshmallows

snip on diagonal

coated spines

2 Build shape

mound frosting

add Kiss near edge

3 Attach spines

add in rows

pointed-ends up, facing Kiss

leave room for eyes

4 Add face

Sixlet eye

frosting

pearl nose

137

MY PAD OR YOURS?

small jelly beans

blue frosting

sprinkles

stick gum

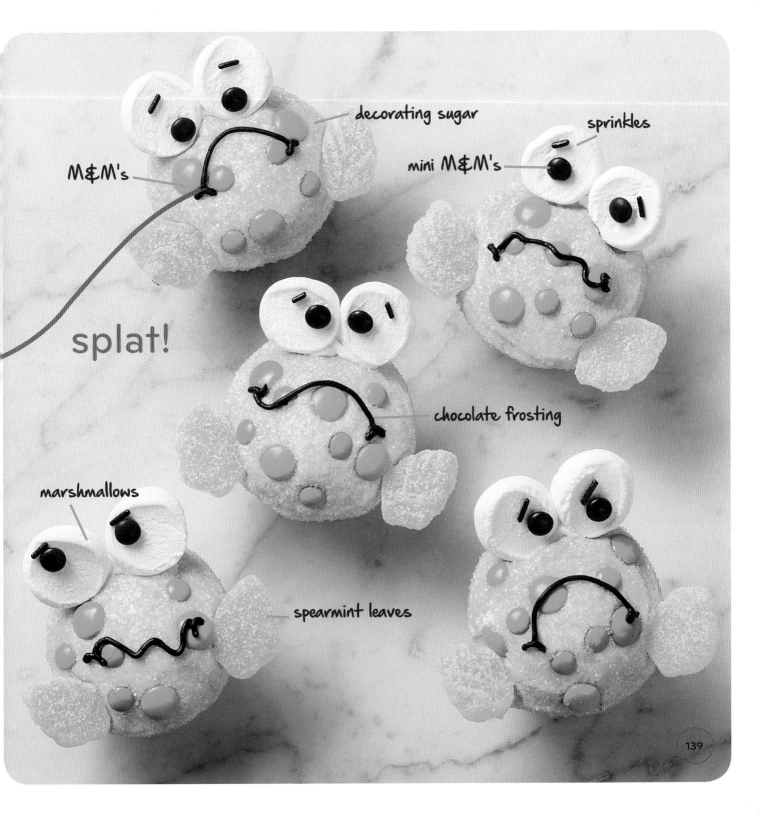

decorating sugar

sprinkles

mini M&M's

M&M's

splat!

chocolate frosting

marshmallows

spearmint leaves

139

FROGS

12 vanilla cupcakes, chilled
8 marshmallows
24 brown M&M's Minis
24 chocolate sprinkles
12 spearmint leaf candies
48 thin pretzel sticks
1 (16-ounce) can vanilla frosting
¼ cup dark chocolate frosting
72 green M&M's Minis
60 green M&M's
1¼ cups light green decorating sugar, such as Wilton

1. Snip the marshmallows crosswise into thirds. Reshape the slices into circles and place in pairs on a sheet of waxed paper, sticky-side up. For the eyes, add brown mini M&M's and chocolate sprinkles to each pair, making matching expressions.
2. For the legs, slice each spearmint leaf in half through the side. Place the 24 leaf shapes, sticky-side up, all oriented with the pointy end up, in pairs on a sheet of waxed paper. Press the end of a pretzel stick into each leaf, with one pretzel in each pair pointing to the right and one to the left.
3. Spoon ¼ cup of the vanilla frosting into a zip-top bag and ¼ cup of the dark chocolate frosting into a separate bag. Working on one cupcake at a time to prevent the frosting from drying, spread a mound of the remaining vanilla frosting on top and smooth. Press a few mini and regular green M&M's on top. Put the decorating sugar in a bowl and roll the top of the cupcake in the sugar to coat. Gently pat to reshape. Brush the M&M's to remove excess sugar. Repeat with the remaining cupcakes.
4. To support the eyes, insert 2 pretzel sticks into the top edge of the cupcakes about ½ inch apart and overhanging the edge by ½ inch. Snip a small corner from the bags of frosting. Pipe vanilla frosting on the pretzels and on the cupcake between them, and attach the marshmallow eyes. Add a pair of legs to each cupcake, one on each side, by pushing the pretzels into the frosting. Pipe lines of dark chocolate frosting for the mouths.

Makes 12 cupcakes

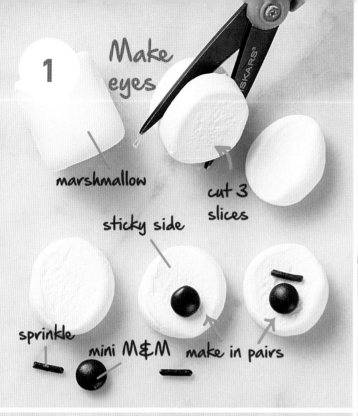

1 Make eyes

marshmallow

cut 3 slices

sticky side

sprinkle

mini M&M

make in pairs

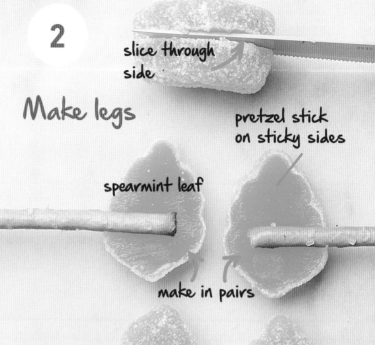

2 slice through side

Make legs

spearmint leaf

pretzel stick on sticky sides

make in pairs

3 Sugarcoat skin

mound frosting

mini M&M & M&M warts

decorating sugar

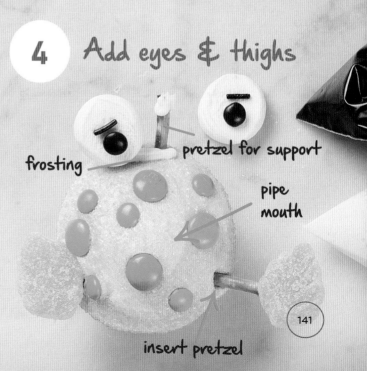

4 Add eyes & thighs

frosting

pretzel for support

pipe mouth

insert pretzel

141

DRAGONFLIES

12 vanilla cupcakes, chilled
24 sticks yellow gum, such as Juicy Fruit
48 small pearlized jelly beans, such as Jelly Belly
1 (16-ounce) can vanilla frosting
Neon blue food coloring, such as McCormick
48 small colored sprinkles, such as Wilton

1. For the wings, make a diagonal cut to remove one
   third from each stick of gum to make 24 large and 24
   small pieces. Use small scissors to shape the pieces
   into large and small wings.
2. Use a small knife to cut 24 of the jelly beans in half
   crosswise.
3. Spoon ¼ cup of the frosting into a zip-top bag.
   Tint the remaining frosting pale blue with the food
   coloring. Spread some of the blue frosting on top of
   each cupcake and smooth. Insert a small wing into
   the frosting near the center of the cupcake and add
   a large wing next to it. Arrange another set of wings
   close together, opposite the first set.
4. For the body, press a whole jelly bean, lengthwise, at
   the center of the cupcake, between the wings. Add
   the head, crosswise, between the large wings. For
   the tail, place 4 halved jelly beans in a line extending
   beyond the small wings, cut-side down. Snip a very
   small corner from the bag of vanilla frosting. Pipe
   small dots of frosting on the head and add sprinkles
   for the eyes.

Makes 12 cupcakes

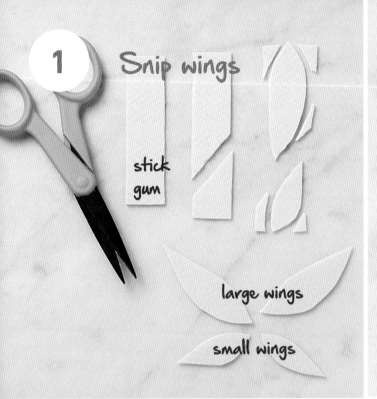

1 Snip wings

stick gum

large wings

small wings

2 Cut body

small jelly beans

cut in half

3 Attach wings

small wing

push into frosting

large wing

4 Make faces

cut jelly beans

frosting

whole jelly beans

sprinkle eye

143

Wing It!

Candy, cookies, and snacks give wing to insects, birds, bees, and even fairies. Let your imagination soar!

heart-shaped candy

fruit slices

Jordan almonds

Vienna Fingers

fruit leather

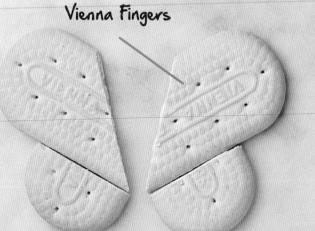

Nitwitz Kooky Bananas

orange
fruit
slices

Golden Oreo
Thins

mini pretzels

Big Red gum

Juicy Fruit gum

marshmallows

WE WISH YOU A MERRY CUPCAKE
Year-round holiday-licious decorating ideas!

LOVE IS
IN THE AIR!

red licorice laces

marshmallows

milk chocolate frosting

Hershey's Kiss

Hershey's Kiss

Spree

blue sprinkles

red sprinkle

red frosting

3 hearts + Spree = flower

149

VALENTINE LOVEBUGS

12 strawberry cupcakes, chilled
6 marshmallows
6 strands red licorice lace, such as Twizzlers Pull'n'Peel
1 cup milk chocolate frosting
1 (16-ounce) can vanilla frosting
Neon pink food coloring, such as McCormick
24 chocolate Hershey's Kisses
24 blue sprinkles, such as Wilton
12 red sprinkles, such as Wilton

1. For the wings, snip each marshmallow crosswise into 4 slices. For the antennae, cut the red laces into twenty-four 2-inch pieces.
2. Spoon the milk chocolate frosting into a zip-top bag and ¼ cup of the vanilla frosting into a separate bag. Snip a small corner from the bag with the vanilla frosting, and a ¼-inch corner from the bag with the chocolate frosting. Tint the remaining vanilla frosting pink with the food coloring. Spread some of the pink frosting on top of the cupcakes and smooth. For the body, use the chocolate frosting to pipe a row of four overlapping ¾-inch dots down the center of each cupcake.
3. Place a chocolate Kiss at the front of the frosting body, pointed-end down, for the head and one Kiss at the opposite end, pointed-end up, for the stinger. Press a marshmallow wing into the frosting on either side of the flat-head Kiss.
4. Use vanilla frosting to attach the blue sprinkle eyes and red sprinkle noses. Press 2 licorice lace antennae into the frosting behind the heads.

Makes 12 cupcakes

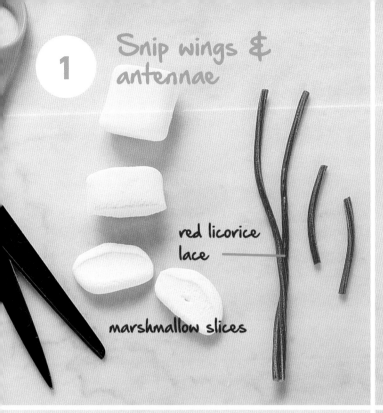

1 Snip wings & antennae

red licorice lace

marshmallow slices

2 Pipe body

four overlapping dots

milk chocolate frosting

3 Add head, tail & wings

chocolate Kisses

pointed end out

wings

pointed end in

4 Make faces

frosting

sprinkle

licorice lace

nose

151

SWEET HEARTS

12 vanilla cupcakes, chilled
12 chocolate Pocky sticks
½ cup dark cocoa melting wafers, such as Wilton
6 Vienna Fingers
1 (16-ounce) can vanilla frosting
Red paste food coloring, such as Wilton

1. For the arrows, cut the Pocky sticks in half and place the 6 pieces with uncoated ends on a cookie sheet lined with waxed paper. Put the dark cocoa melting wafers in a zip-top bag and microwave in 5-second increments, massaging the bag after each, until smooth. Snip a small corner from the bag and pipe 3 or 4 overlapping V-shapes on the uncoated ends of the cookies. For the arrowheads, pipe twelve ½-inch dots of melted candy on the waxed paper, pulling the tip of the bag slightly to one side to make a point. Place the unbroken end of one of the remaining Pocky sticks on top of each wet arrowhead opposite the point. Refrigerate for 5 minutes, until set.

2. Line a second cookie sheet with waxed paper. For the hearts, separate the Vienna Fingers—remove and discard the creme—to make 12 cookies. Use a small serrated knife to saw the cookies crosswise on a slight diagonal, cutting them in half. Flip one piece and place the cut sides together to create the heart shapes. Arrange the hearts on the lined cookie sheet. Reheat the melted candy, if necessary, pipe a line of candy along the cut edges of the cookies, and press together. Refrigerate for 5 minutes, until set.

3. Put ¾ cup of the frosting in a bowl and tint it bright red (or pink) with the paste food coloring. Line a third cookie sheet with waxed paper and set a wire rack over the pan. Arrange the heart cookies on the rack. Put the red frosting in a glass measuring cup and microwave in 4-second intervals, stirring after each, until thinned slightly. Pour the frosting over the cookie hearts to cover them completely. Refrigerate for 30 minutes, until set.

4. Spread the remaining vanilla frosting on top of the cupcakes and smooth. Carefully remove the arrow parts from the waxed paper. Insert an arrowhead and a feather on the top of each cupcake, pushing the broken ends into the frosting, aligned, about 1½ inches apart. Place a cookie heart on top of each arrow.

Makes 12 cupcakes

1 Pipe arrows

arrowhead

pipe dot & pull

cut Pocky

feather

melted candy

overlapping V-shapes

2 Make cookie hearts

remove creme

cut on diagonal

VIENNA FINGER

melted candy

flip one side

melted candy

3 Coat hearts

pour to coat

melted frosting

4 Assemble chilled parts

insert end

line up arrowhead & feather

offset spatula

add heart to center

PESKY WABBITS!

mini gumball

black pearl

pink decorating sugar

small jelly bean

mini marshmallows

white sprinkles

jumbo marshmallows

green apple twists

circus peanut

Oreo crumbs

chocolate
cupcake

155

EASTER BUNNIES

12 vanilla cupcakes, chilled
6 jumbo marshmallows, such as Campfire
½ cup pink decorating sugar, such as Cake Mate
12 mini marshmallows
1 (16-ounce) can vanilla frosting
1½ cups white sprinkles, such as Wilton
24 black pearls, such as SweetWorks
12 small pink jelly beans, such as Jelly Belly
12 pearlized white gumballs, such as SweetWorks

1. For the ears, cut the jumbo marshmallows crosswise into 4 slices. Put the decorating sugar in a bowl and dip one cut side of the marshmallow slices into the sugar to coat. Cut the mini marshmallows in half crosswise for the paws.
2. Spoon ¼ cup of the vanilla frosting into a zip-top bag. Spread a mound of the remaining frosting on top of the cupcakes and smooth. Put the sprinkles in a bowl and roll the tops of the cupcakes in the sprinkles to coat. Gently pat to reshape.
3. Insert the narrow end of 2 marshmallow ears into the frosting, side by side, near the center of the cupcakes, sugar side facing out.
4. Snip a small corner from the bag of frosting. Use dots of frosting to add the pearl eyes, jelly bean nose, and gumball tail. Pipe dots of frosting and attach the mini marshmallow paws, sticky-side down, on the front edge of the cupcakes.

Makes 12 cupcakes

1 Make ears & paws

jumbo marshmallow

4 slices

sticky side

decorating sugar

paw

ear

cut mini marshmallows in half

2 Add rabbit fur

sprinkles

mound frosting

3 Insert ears

push into frosting

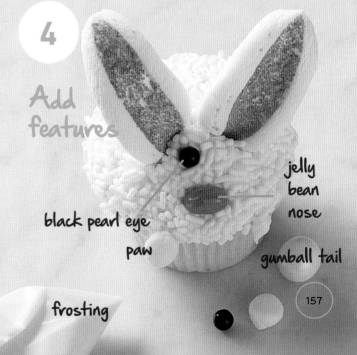

4 Add features

jelly bean nose

black pearl eye

paw

gumball tail

frosting

157

CARROT PATCH

24 chocolate cupcakes, chilled
8 green apple fruit twists, such as Kenny's Candy
  Juicy Twists
24 circus peanuts
1 (16-ounce) can milk chocolate frosting
2 cups Oreo cookie crumbs

1. For the carrot fronds, cut the green twists crosswise
   into thirds. To feather the fronds, cut lengthwise strips
   into one short end of the twists, stopping ½ inch from
   the opposite end.
2. For the carrots, lightly pinch and roll one end of
   the circus peanuts between your fingers to make
   a pointed shape. Using a toothpick, make a small
   opening for the fronds at the wide end of the carrots. Slightly
   taper the uncut end of each candy frond. Wet the tapered end
   with a drop of water and press it into the opening at the wide end
   of each circus peanut.
3. Use a small knife or an apple corer to remove a ¾-inch diameter
   circle, about 1¼ inches deep, from the center of each cupcake.
4. Spoon the milk chocolate frosting into two separate zip-top bags
   (smaller bags are easier to handle). Snip a ¼-inch corner from
   the bags. Pipe frosting on top of the cupcakes to cover all but
   the opening. Put the cookie crumbs in a bowl and roll the tops of
   the cupcakes in the crumbs to coat. Gently pat to reshape. Insert
   a carrot into the openings. Add more cookie crumbs as dirt, if
   desired.

Makes 24 cupcakes

1 Cut carrot tops

cut twists

make fringe

do not cut through end

2 Make carrots

water

make hole with toothpick

add dot of water

insert frond

shape circus peanut

taper ends

3 Dig hole

remove cake

apple corer or knife

4 Add garden soil

pipe milk chocolate frosting

leave hole open

insert carrot

roll in crumbs

159

BIG BANG!

yellow gumdrop

blue decorating spray

marshmallows

red licorice laces

red decorating spray

yellow decorating sugar

red Twizzlers

Sixlets

blue Twizzlers

frosting

PATRIOTIC ROCKETS

12 vanilla cupcakes, chilled

½ cup yellow decorating sugar, such as Cake Mate

12 large yellow gumdrops

36 marshmallows

12 long thin pretzel sticks or Pringles Stix cookie sticks, any sweet flavor

2 cans (1.5 ounces each) Wilton decorating spray, 1 red and 1 blue

12 strands red licorice lace, such as Twizzlers Pull'n'Peel

½ cup white melting wafers, such as Wilton

1 (16-ounce) can vanilla frosting

1. Sprinkle your work surface with some decorating sugar. Roll out the gumdrops, one at a time, adding more sugar to prevent sticking, into 2-inch rounds. Use a 1¾-inch cutter to make 12 circles.

2. Remove a one-third wedge from each circle and press the sticky edges together to make 12 nose cones.

3. Gently thread a marshmallow onto one end of each pretzel stick, pushing ½ inch of the pretzel through the opposite side of the marshmallow, and place on a sheet of waxed paper. Spray with the red decorating spray to coat and let dry. Insert 12 marshmallows onto toothpicks and place them on the waxed paper. Spray with the blue decorating spray and let dry. Spray all of the marshmallows again, using the same colors, to intensify the shade; let dry.

4. To assemble the rockets, carefully thread a white marshmallow onto each pretzel up to the red marshmallow. Remove the toothpick

from the blue marshmallows and carefully thread one onto each pretzel up to the white marshmallows. To make the rocket flames, cut the red laces into 3-inch pieces. Pinch the ends of 3 pieces together. Put the melting wafers in a zip-top bag and microwave in 5-second intervals, massaging the bag after each, until smooth. Snip a small corner from the bag. Pipe a dot of melted candy on both extended ends of the pretzels. Add a yellow candy nosepiece to the red marshmallow ends and red flames to the blue marshmallow end. Refrigerate for 5 minutes, until set. Spread the top of each cupcake with vanilla frosting and smooth. Arrange a rocket on top of each cupcake, pressing them into the frosting to secure.

Makes 12 cupcakes

162

1 Roll nosecone

gumdrop

cut circle

flatten gumdrop

yellow decorating sugar

2 Shape nosecone

discard

remove one-third

press cut edges together

cone shape

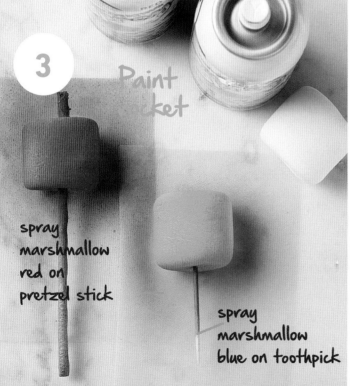

3 Paint rocket

spray marshmallow red on pretzel stick

spray marshmallow blue on toothpick

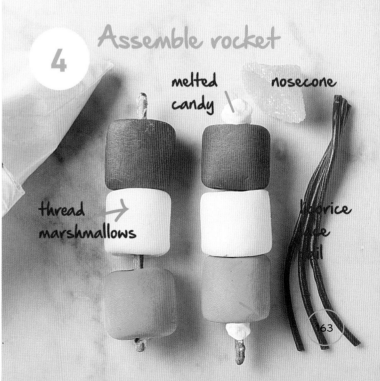

4 Assemble rocket

melted candy

nosecone

thread marshmallows

licorice lace tail

163

FOURTH OF JULY EXPLOSIONS

12 vanilla cupcakes, chilled
10 blue and red Twizzlers licorice twists (5 blue and 5 red)
1 (16-ounce) can vanilla frosting
½ cup white pearlized Sixlets, such as SweetWorks

1. Use scissors to snip the red and blue twists on an angle into very thin slices.
2. Working on one cupcake at a time to prevent drying, spread some frosting on top and smooth. To make the blast patterns, start with an outer ring of one color of the sliced candy, placed close together, in the frosting.
3. Add a second ring inside and overlapping the first ring using a different color sliced candy. Continue with the remaining cupcakes, varying the blast patterns and placement on each cupcake.
4. Arrange several Sixlets in the center of each explosion.

Makes 12 cupcakes

1 Snip twists

Twizzlers

cut on diagonal

thin slices

2 Make blast

side by side
outer ring

frosting

3 Add to pattern

overlap
outer
ring

alternate colors

4 Add sparkle to center

pearlized
Sixlets

165

TRICK OR
TREATS!

black pearls

Smarties

yellow frosting

Nabisco Famous
Chocolate Wafers

dark chocolate frosting

marshmallow

candy-
coated
pretzels

circus peanut

orange
frosting

166

chocolate
frosting

Utz Honey
Wheat Twists

167

HALLOWEEN BATS

12 chocolate cupcakes, chilled
12 Nabisco Famous Chocolate Wafers
1 (16-ounce) can vanilla frosting
Yellow food coloring, such as McCormick
1 cup dark chocolate frosting
24 yellow or orange Smarties
24 black pearls, such as SweetWorks

1. Microwave 1 chocolate wafer at a time for 10 to 15 seconds each to soften. Cut the cookie in half to make 2 wings. Use a small cutter or pastry tip to scallop the wings by removing two adjacent ¾-inch circular segments from one end of the cut edge. Discard the scraps.

2. Spoon 2 tablespoons of the vanilla frosting into a zip-top bag and the dark chocolate frosting into a separate bag. Tint the remaining vanilla frosting bright yellow with the food coloring. Spread some of the yellow frosting on top of the cupcakes and smooth. Snip a ½-inch corner from the bag of dark chocolate frosting. Pipe a 1½-inch dollop on top of the cupcakes to make the bat bodies.

3. Insert the cookie wings, round-edge up and pointed-end out, into the frosting on either side of the bat bodies.

4. For the eyes, add two Smarties to the center of the chocolate bodies. Snip a small corner from the bag of vanilla frosting, pipe dots of the frosting on the Smarties, and add the black pearls.

Makes 12 cupcakes

1 Cut wings

cut in half

scallop flat edge

small cutter

2 Pipe bat body

dollop of dark chocolate frosting

yellow frosting

3 rounded edge up

Add wings

pointed end out

4 Add eyes

Smarties

frosting

black pearl

PRETZEL SKELETONS

12 chocolate cupcakes, chilled
12 marshmallows
12 long thin pretzel sticks
48 yogurt- or white candy–coated mini pretzel twists
1 (16-ounce) can dark chocolate frosting

1. For the skulls, snip a ¼-inch-wide strip lengthwise from the rounded side of each marshmallow, reserving the strips. Remove a second strip from the opposite side of the marshmallows to narrow the skulls. Place the skulls flat-side down and insert a pretzel stick into one of the rounded ends. For the neck bones, cut ¼ inch from the reserved marshmallow strips and press the piece, sticky-side down, onto the pretzel where it meets the skull. Trim 1 inch from the end of each pretzel and set aside.

2. Use a small serrated knife to saw the bottom loop from the coated pretzels. (Reserve the bottom pieces for the arms and legs.) Use the attached top loops for the ribs. (There will be 12 extra ribs in case of breakage.)

3. Spoon ¼ cup of the dark chocolate frosting into a zip-top bag. Spread some of the remaining frosting on top of the cupcakes and smooth. Shingle 3 ribs, overlapping slightly, cut-side down, in the center of the cupcakes. For the arms, press 2 trimmed pretzel pieces into the frosting on either side of the top ribs, overhanging the edge. For the legs, add 2 more trimmed pieces below the bottom ribs, overhanging the edge.

4. To attach the skulls, insert a pretzel end into the top edge of each cupcake just above the ribs, until the neck bone touches the frosting. Snip a small corner from the bag of frosting. Pipe dots of chocolate frosting as the eyes, nose, and mouth on the skulls.

Makes 12 cupcakes

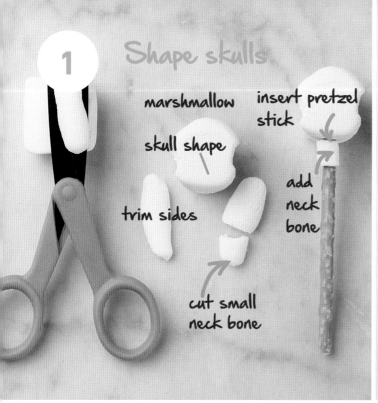

1 Shape skulls

marshmallow

skull shape

trim sides

cut small neck bone

insert pretzel stick

add neck bone

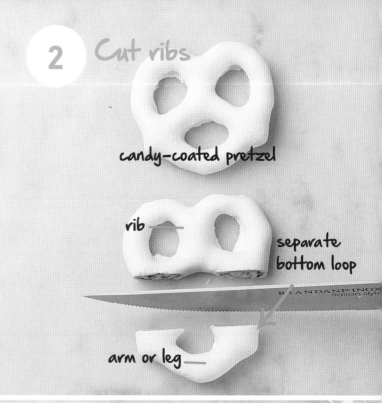

2 Cut ribs

candy-coated pretzel

rib

separate bottom loop

arm or leg

BLANDANI INOX *Italian Style*

3 Build bones

cut side into frosting

arm

row of ribs

leg

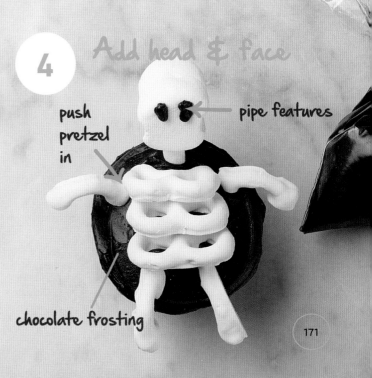

4 Add head & face

push pretzel in

pipe features

chocolate frosting

171

CIRCUS PEANUT PUMPKINS

12 spice cupcakes, chilled
6 Utz Honey Wheat Twists
12 circus peanuts
1 (16-ounce) can vanilla frosting
Yellow and red food coloring, such as McCormick

1. For the stems, use a small serrated knife to saw 1 inch from each end of the wheat twists; discard the centers.
2. For the skin, place the circus peanuts on their side and cut in half lengthwise. Working on one slice at a time, roll out each piece to a 1½ by 3-inch rectangle. (It will be very thin.) Keep the slices covered with plastic wrap to prevent drying out.
3. For the candy ribs, use scissors to cut each rolled rectangle in half lengthwise. Trim the pieces into long narrow leaf shapes with pointed ends. (It's okay for each piece to be a little different.) Keep the slices covered to prevent drying out.
4. Tint the vanilla frosting orange with the yellow and red food coloring. Spread a mound of frosting on top of the cupcakes and smooth. Use a clean offset spatula and swipe the frosting in one direction four or five times to create parallel lines. (Make sure to wipe the spatula clean after each swipe.) Loosely attach the ends of 4 of the candy ribs to align with the frosting swipes, taking care not to press them flat into the frosting. For the stem, insert the cut end of the wheat twists at the top edge of the cupcakes.

Makes 12 cupcakes

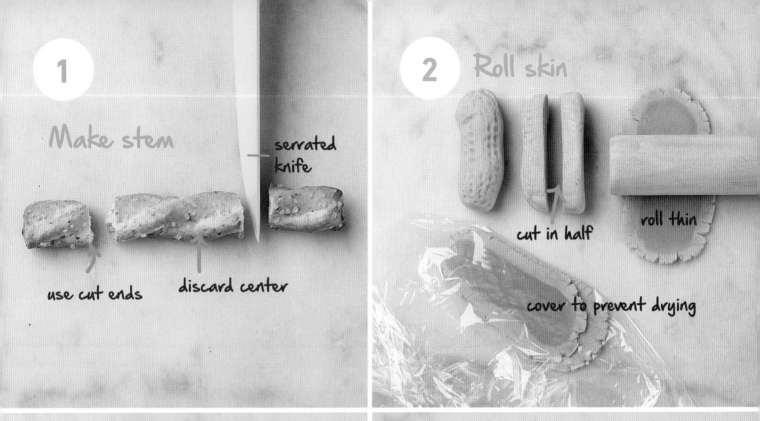

1 Make stem

serrated knife

use cut ends

discard center

2 Roll skin

cut in half

roll thin

cover to prevent drying

3 Carve pumpkin ribs

2 leaf-shaped ribs from each slice

keep covered

FISKARS

4 Shape pumpkin

insert stem

mound of frosting

parallel swipes in frosting

loosely attach

173

MONSTER MOUTHS

12 chocolate cupcakes, chilled
6 large black gumdrops
6 marshmallows
72 mini marshmallows
¾ cup vanilla frosting
Red food coloring, such as McCormick
1 (16-ounce) can caramel frosting
24 banana Runts

1. For the nose, place the gumdrops flat-side down and cut them in half. Place each half sticky-side down on a sheet of waxed paper. Use a large straw to punch out nostrils on either side of the round edge, about ¼ inch apart. For the large fangs, snip triangles, about 1 inch long by ½ inch wide, from the regular marshmallows, cutting through the curved end and along the sides. For the small fangs, snip 12 of the mini marshmallows in half on an angle.

2. Spoon ¼ cup of the vanilla frosting into a zip-top bag. Tint the remaining vanilla frosting red with the food coloring. Spread an oval shape of red frosting, about 1½ inches by 2½ inches, on the center of each cupcake and smooth. Spoon the remaining red frosting into a zip-top bag. For the teeth, press 3 uncut mini marshmallows into the lower edge of the oval and 2 into the upper edge, leaving about ¾ inch between the uppers and lowers. Snip a small corner from the bag of vanilla frosting. Using dots of the frosting as needed, attach 2 large fangs on the outer edge of the top teeth and 2 mini fangs on the bottom row of teeth.

3. For the fur, divide the caramel frosting between two zip-top bags (smaller bags are easier to handle). Snip small corners from the bags. Starting along the bottom edge of the cupcakes, pipe two overlapping rows of frosting dots, pulling away from the mouth, up to the edge of the teeth. Continue piping around the sides of the mouth, always pulling away from the teeth.

4. Pipe a row of fur frosting above the mouth, pulling down and slightly overlapping the top teeth. Continue to add overlapping rows of fur to cover the cupcakes. Add the banana Runts on the top row of teeth as the yellow fangs. Snip a very small corner from the bag of red frosting. Pipe a small amount of red frosting on the marshmallow fangs for blood. Press a gumdrop nose into the frosting near the top edge of the cupcakes.

Makes 12 cupcakes

1 Cut nose & fangs

- gumdrop
- marshmallow
- mini marshmallow
- side cut
- diagonal cut
- split
- nostril
- large straw
- large fang
- small fangs

2 Assemble teeth

- mini marshmallows
- frosting
- top row
- large fang
- red frosting
- bottom row
- small fang

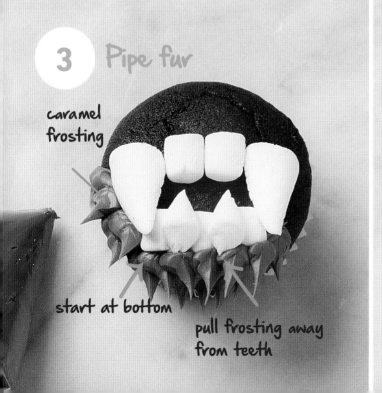

3 Pipe fur

- caramel frosting
- start at bottom
- pull frosting away from teeth

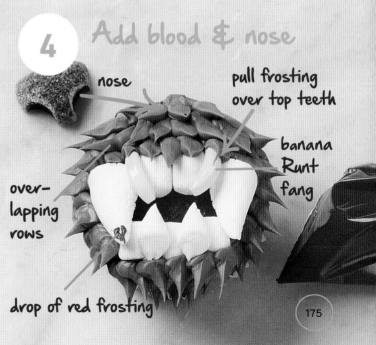

4 Add blood & nose

- nose
- pull frosting over top teeth
- over-lapping rows
- banana Runt fang
- drop of red frosting

175

SPIDER BITES!

Oreo crumbs

mini Oreo

Nitwitz Kooky Bananas

decorating sugar

crumb-coated Twizzlers Pull'n'Peel

M&M's

sprinkles

frosting

CUPCAKE SPIDERS

12 chocolate cupcakes, chilled

1 (16-ounce) can vanilla frosting

1 cup decorating sugar, any color, such as Cake Mate

½ cup dark cocoa melting wafers, such as Wilton

½ cup M&M's, color to match sugar

½ cup Nitwitz Kooky Bananas, color to match sugar, such as SweetWorks

48 strands red licorice lace, Twizzlers Pull'n'Peel

30 Oreo Minis

48 sprinkles, color to match sugar, such as Wilton

1. For the legs, place 18 mini Oreos in a food processor and pulse into fine crumbs. Pour the crumbs into a bowl. Cut the licorice laces into ninety-six 4½-inch-long pieces. Line a cookie sheet with waxed paper. Put the melting wafers in a small bowl and microwave in 5-second increments, stirring after each, until smooth. Dip all but ½ inch of a licorice piece in the melted candy to coat. Allow the excess candy to drip back into the bowl and drop the wet strand into the bowl of cookie crumbs to coat. Transfer the legs to the lined cookie sheet and shape into a curve. Refrigerate until set.

2. Spoon ¼ cup of vanilla frosting into a zip-top bag. Mound some of the remaining vanilla frosting on top of the cupcakes and smooth. Put the decorating sugar (your choice of color) in a bowl and roll the tops of the cupcakes in the sugar to coat. Gently pat to reshape.

3. For the head, snip a small corner from the bag of vanilla frosting and pipe a dot of frosting near one edge of each cupcake. Attach a mini Oreo to the frosting. For the eyes, pipe 4 small dots of frosting on top of the Oreo and add sprinkles. For the pinchers, insert 2 banana candies under the head, pressing them into the frosting to secure. Press 2 M&M's into the frosting on top of the cupcake in a row behind the head.

4. Snip the red ends from the chilled legs. To assemble, place the cupcakes on a serving platter. Use a toothpick to poke 4 small holes on either side of the cupcakes, close to the edge, and insert the cut end of a candy leg in each hole.

Makes 12 spiders

Make It Even Easier! Use Oreo Crumbs for the Legs AND the Body.

1 Dip & coat legs

melted candy

Oreo crumbs

Twizzlers Pull'n'Peel

shape legs

2 Sugarcoat

mound frosting

decorating sugar

3 Add head & spots

M&M spot

mini Oreo head

frosting

sprinkle eyes

Nitwitz Kooky Banana fangs

4 Add legs

toothpick hole

insert leg

snip off end

179 SKARS

GOBBLE, GOBBLE, GOBBLE!

candy corn

Ferrero Rocher chocolate

thin chocolate cookie

sprinkles

Fruit by the Foot

spice cupcake

milk chocolate frosting

Nitwitz Kooky Banana

food coloring

cornflake marshmallow treats

pretzel rod

THANKSGIVING TURKEYS

12 spice cupcakes, chilled

12 chocolate Maria cookies, such as Goya

¼ cup vanilla frosting

1 (16-ounce) can milk chocolate frosting

84 pieces candy corn

12 thin pretzel sticks

12 Ferrero Rocher candies

4 inches strawberry fruit leather, such as Fruit by the Foot

12 orange Nitwitz Kooky Bananas

24 purple sprinkles, such as Wilton

1. For the tail, use a small serrated knife to saw a ¾-inch piece from one side of the chocolate cookies. Saw the trimmed piece in half crosswise to make the wings.

2. Spoon the vanilla frosting into a zip-top bag and ½ cup of the milk chocolate frosting into a separate bag. Snip a small corner from the bag of chocolate frosting. For the tail feathers, pipe a line of the milk chocolate frosting along the rounded edge of the large cookie pieces and attach 7 pieces of candy corn, flat ends at the edge of the cookie. Spread a mound of the remaining milk chocolate frosting on top of the cupcakes and smooth. To support the tail, insert a pretzel stick near one edge of each cupcake, leaving 1 inch exposed.

3. Pipe a dot of milk chocolate frosting on the end of the exposed pretzel. Add a tail feather cookie to the cupcakes, pressing the cut side into the frosting, and leaning against the pretzel. For the head, press the Ferrero Rocher candy into the frosting in front of the tail. Insert the pointed end of the small cookie wings on either side of the head.

4. For the wattle, cut the fruit leather into ½-inch tear drop shapes. For the beak, cut the banana candies in half. Snip a small corner from the bag of vanilla frosting. Pipe dots of vanilla frosting on the head and attach the sprinkle eyes, banana beak, and fruit leather wattle.

Makes 12 cupcakes

1 Cut tail & wings

cut off one-third

tail

cut in half

wing

chocolate cookie

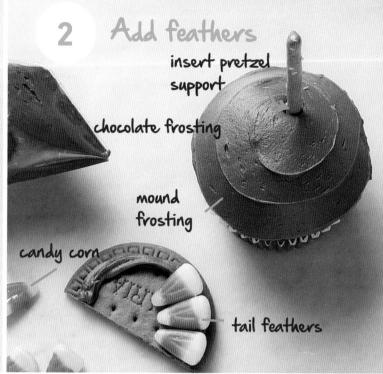

2 Add feathers

insert pretzel support

chocolate frosting

mound frosting

candy corn

tail feathers

3 Attach head, tail & wings

cookie upright against pretzel

Ferrero Rocher candy

insert narrow end

4 Make faces

sprinkle eye

banana candy beak

fruit roll wattle

frosting

183

AUTUMN LEAVES

24 vanilla cupcakes, chilled
6 cups mini marshmallows
6 tablespoons butter
6 cups cornflakes
Red, green, and yellow food coloring, such as McCor-
    mick
1 (16-ounce) can caramel or milk chocolate frosting
12 pretzel rods

1. For the leaves, put 1½ cups of the mini marshmallows
   and 1½ tablespoons of the butter in a medium bowl
   and microwave, stirring frequently, until melted. Tint
   the mixture using one color of the food coloring. Add
   1½ cups of the cornflakes and fold gently to coat the
   cereal completely.

2. Spread the tinted cereal mixture in a thin layer of small
   clusters on a sheet of waxed paper to cool. Repeat Step 1 to
   make leaves in three additional colors. (Use red and yellow
   food coloring to make orange.)

3. Spread the top of the cupcakes with some frosting and
   smooth. For the tree trunks, break the pretzel rods in half
   crosswise. Press the cut end of a pretzel rod into the frosting,
   allowing the uncut end to overhang the edge by 2 inches.

4. Press small clusters of colored cereal leaves on top of the
   cupcakes, mixing the colors as desired and using additional
   frosting as needed to secure.

Makes 24 trees

1 Tint leaves

cornflakes

melted marshmallow

food coloring

coat evenly

2

small clusters

Spread & cool

waxed paper

3 Add trunk

press into frosting

caramel frosting

overhang 2 inches

finished end

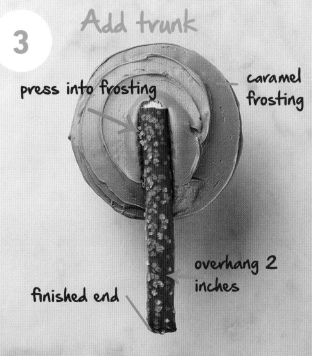

4 Attach clusters

press into frosting

mix colors

185

Turn Over a New Leaf!

Marshmallow treats can be made from almost any cereal. And each new shape grows a different tree.

Kix

Rice Krispies

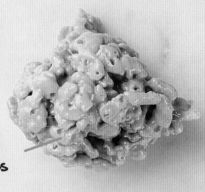

Rice Krispies

Honeycomb

puffed millet

Cocoa Puffs

puffed rice

cereal stars

Cheerios

Cap'n
Crunch

Life cereal

SANTA'S GOT A CREW!

mini M&M's

mini marshmallows

Anna's Swedish Thins

decorating sugar

Smarties

small jelly bean

Smartie

melting wafers

mini marshmallows

pretzel

sprinkles

Grasshopper cookie

mini M&M

jelly bean

SANTA FACE

12 vanilla cupcakes, chilled
1 cup white melting wafers, such as Wilton
12 thin ginger cookies, Anna's Swedish Thins
12 small pink jelly beans, such as Jelly Belly
1 cup mini marshmallows
1 (16-ounce) can vanilla frosting
24 white Smarties
24 blue M&M's Minis
1¾ cups red decorating sugar, such as Cake Mate
12 pink Smarties

1. Line a cookie sheet with waxed paper. For the beard, put the melting wafers in a small bowl and microwave in 5-second increments, stirring after each, until smooth. Brush any excess crumbs from the cookies. Spoon a smooth coat of the melted candy over the cookies, leaving two scallops uncovered. Allow the excess candy to drip back into the bowl. Transfer to the lined cookie sheet. For the nose, add a jelly bean to the wet candy just below the uncoated scallops. Refrigerate until set, about 5 minutes.

2. For the mustache and eyebrows, snip 24 of the marshmallows in half on an angle. Spoon ½ cup of the vanilla frosting into a zip-top bag. Snip a small corner from the bag of frosting. For the eyes, pipe dots of the frosting on the white Smarties and attach the blue mini M&M's.

3. Frost the tops of the cupcakes with a mound of the remaining frosting and smooth. Put the decorating sugar in a bowl and roll the tops of the cupcakes in the sugar to coat. Gently pat to reshape.

4. Pipe some frosting on each cupcake, slightly off center, and attach a cookie beard to one side, with the uncoated scallops positioned near the center of the cupcake. Pipe dots of frosting on the two uncoated scallops and add a white Smarties eye to each. Pipe dots of frosting and add the pink Smarties mouth below the nose, the marshmallow mustache pieces between the nose and mouth, and the marshmallow eyebrows on top of the sugar above the eyes. For the pom-poms, use dots of frosting to attach whole marshmallows next to the beards.

Makes 12 cupcakes

190

1 Candy-coat beard

make coating smooth

melted candy

2 scallops uncoated

add nose to wet candy

2 Make features

mini M&M's

cut on diagonal

add frosting to Smarties eyes

mustache & brow

3 Sugarcoat

mound frosting

pat to reshape

decorating sugar

4 Assemble

frosting

jelly bean nose

Smartie mouth

mini marshmallow pom-pom

191

REINDEER ROUNDUP

12 chocolate cupcakes, chilled
12 thin pretzel twists
¼ cup vanilla frosting
1 (16-ounce) can chocolate frosting
1½ cups chocolate sprinkles, such as Cake Mate
12 Grasshopper cookies
11 black jelly beans
1 red jelly bean
36 brown M&M's Minis

1. For the antlers, use a small serrated knife to gently saw each pretzel twist in half. Remove and discard the center knot to make 2 mirror-image antlers.
2. Spoon the vanilla frosting into a zip-top bag and ¼ cup of the chocolate frosting into a separate bag. Spread a mound of the remaining chocolate frosting on top of the cupcakes and smooth. Put the chocolate sprinkles in a bowl and roll the tops of the cupcakes in the sprinkles to coat. Gently pat to reshape.
3. Snip a small corner from the bags of frosting. Pipe some chocolate frosting on the cupcakes, slightly off center, and add the cookie muzzle to one side. Pipe dots of chocolate frosting on the cookies and attach a jelly bean nose and mini M&M mouth. For the eyes, pipe dots of vanilla frosting on the cupcakes above the cookie muzzle and add brown mini M&M's.
4. Insert the pretzel antlers, rounded-sides out, about 2 inches apart at the top edge of the cupcakes.

Makes 12 cupcakes

1 Make antlers

remove center knot

use gentle sawing motion

cut bottom loop

pretzel twist

mirror-image antlers

2 Sprinkle coat

chocolate sprinkles

mound frosting

3 Add features

mini M&M eye

jelly bean nose

frosting

mouth

Grasshopper cookie

chocolate frosting

4 Attach antlers

insert pretzel

193

mini doughnut wreaths

Hubba Bubba
Bubble Tape

frosting

pearls

WREATH!

green frosting

pearls

Fruit by the Foot

mini doughnut wreaths

MINI CHRISTMAS WREATH CUPCAKES

8 vanilla cupcakes, chilled
1 (.75-ounce) roll strawberry fruit leather, such as
  Fruit by the Foot
4 mini plain or powdered doughnuts, such as Entenmann's
1 (16-ounce) can vanilla frosting
Green and yellow food coloring, such as McCormick
64 to 72 red pearls, such as SweetWorks

1. For the bows, cut the fruit roll into eight 1¾-inch
   pieces and twenty-four ½-inch pieces. For the tails,
   cut a notch from one short end of the 16 small pieces.
   Pinch the larger pieces in the middle and wrap one of
   the remaining small pieces around the pinched area
   to make the bow shape.
2. Brush any excess powdered sugar from the
   doughnuts. Use a small serrated knife to cut the
   doughnuts in half through the side to make 8 circles.
3. Tint 1 cup of the vanilla frosting bright green with
   the green and yellow food coloring. Spoon the green
   frosting into a zip-top bag. Spread a thin layer of the
   remaining vanilla frosting on top of the cupcakes and
   smooth. Press a sliced doughnut, cut-side down, on
   top, pressing it into the frosting. Snip a small corner
   from the bag of green frosting. Pipe swirling lines of
   green frosting to completely cover the doughnuts to
   make the wreaths.
4. Decorate the wreaths with 8 or 9 red pearls. Place a
   red bow close to one edge of each mini wreath. Add
   2 tail pieces below the center of each bow, notched
   ends out. Arrange the mini wreaths on a platter into
   the shape of a larger wreath.

Makes 8 cupcakes

VARIATION:

For a white wreath, use pale blue frosting on top of the
cupcakes, white frosting for the swirls, blue Hubba Bubba
Bubble Tape for the bows, and blue pearls for the decorations.

1 Tie the knot

Fruit by the Foot

pinch in middle

notch in tail

wrap center

2 Shape wreath

brush excess sugar

slice in half

cut-side down

frosting

3 Pipe greenery

small hole

green frosting

completely cover with swirls

4 Decorate

pearls

add bow

gingersnap

frosting

mini M&M's

gingersnap crumbs

graham sticks

GINGERSNAP BABIES

12 spice cupcakes, chilled
48 graham sticks
½ cup vanilla frosting
12 gingersnaps
½ cup red and green M&M's Minis
1 (16-ounce) can caramel frosting
1 cup ground gingersnaps
12 thin pretzel sticks

1. For the arms and legs, use a small serrated knife to saw ½ inch from one short end of each graham stick.

2. Spoon the vanilla frosting into a zip-top bag. Snip a small corner from the bag. Pipe eyes, smiles, and rickrack hair on the gingersnaps, adding 2 red mini M&M's as cheeks. Pipe rickrack cuffs near the uncut ends of the arms and legs.

3. Spread a mound of the caramel frosting on top of each cupcake and smooth. Put the gingersnap crumbs in a bowl and roll the tops of the cupcakes in the crumbs to coat. Gently pat to reshape.

4. Insert a pretzel stick into the top edge of each cupcake, leaving 1 inch of the pretzel exposed as a support for the head. Pipe a dot of frosting on the pretzel sticks. Add a cookie head to each cupcake, pressing the bottom edge into the frosting and resting the cookie on the pretzel. Press the cut ends of the arms and legs at the sides of the cupcakes into the frosting to secure. Pipe dots of frosting to the belly and attach the green and red mini M&M's as buttons.

Makes 12 cupcakes

200

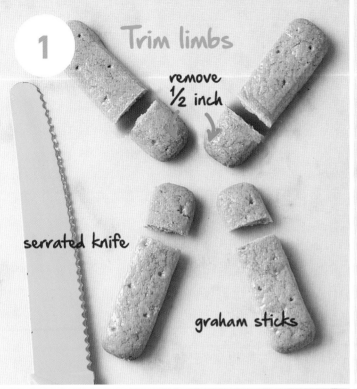

1 Trim limbs

remove ½ inch

serrated knife

graham sticks

2 Pipe details

rickrack hair

gingersnap

frosting

small hole

mini M&M cheeks

rickrack cuffs

3 Crumb coat

mound caramel frosting

gingersnap crumbs

pat to reshape

4 Assemble babies

attach mini M&M buttons

pretzel head support

frosting

insert limbs

201

SNOW DAY!

Crow gumdrop

mini Oreo

circus peanut

marshmallow

dark chocolate frosting

pretzel sticks

Fruit by the Foot

jumbo marshmallow

mini M&M's

frosting

pearl

Laffy Taffy

pretzel

mini Nutter Butters

Change Your Hat-titude!

sprinkle

gumdrop

M&M

Oreo

mini Oreo

mini vanilla wafer

Starlight candy

mini M&M

butter cookie

mega M&M

After Eight mint

Reese's Peanut Butter Cup

203

SNOWMAN CUPCAKES

12 vanilla cupcakes, chilled
6 jumbo marshmallows, such as Campfire
18 marshmallows
1 circus peanut
6 Oreos

1 (16-ounce) can vanilla frosting
¼ cup dark chocolate frosting
12 Oreo Minis
12 red M&M's
1 (.75-ounce) roll strawberry fruit leather, such as Fruit by the Foot
36 blue M&M's Minis

1. For the bodies, cut the jumbo marshmallows in half, end to end, and set aside. Cut 6 of the regular marshmallows in half, end to end. Cut each of the regular marshmallow halves in half again lengthwise to make 24 arms.

2. For the hat, separate the large Oreos—remove and discard the creme—to make 12 cookies. Spoon ½ cup of vanilla frosting into a zip-top bag and the dark chocolate frosting into a separate bag. Snip a very small corner from the bag of chocolate frosting. Pipe a dot of dark chocolate frosting on top of the 12 cookies. Add a whole mini Oreo on top, pressing it into the frosting to secure. Place the circus peanuts on their side and cut in half lengthwise. For the carrot noses, cut each slice crosswise into 6 small triangles.

3. Spread some of the remaining vanilla frosting on top of the cupcakes and smooth. Place a jumbo marshmallow body on top of the cupcakes, cut-side down. Snip a very small corner from the bag of vanilla frosting. Pipe dots of vanilla frosting on the top of the body and attach a marshmallow head, flat side aligned with the flat side of the jumbo marshmallow. Pipe dots of vanilla frosting on the jumbo marshmallow on either side of the head and attach the marshmallow arms. Pipe dots of dark chocolate frosting for the eyes. Pipe a dot of vanilla frosting and add the carrot nose. For the mittens, cut the red M&M's in half and use a dot of vanilla frosting to attach them to the ends of the arms.

4. For the scarf, cut the fruit leather into 2-inch lengths. Cut each piece lengthwise, on a slight angle, to make 2 tapered strips. Remove a notch from the wide end of the fruit leather strips. Insert 2 strips under each marshmallow head, notched ends out and spread apart. Pipe dots of vanilla frosting and add blue mini M&M buttons to the front of the body and the Oreo hat to the top of the head.

Makes 12 cupcakes

1 Shape snow parts

jumbo marshmallow

body

cut in half

regular marshmallow

arms cut in quarters

2 Make hat & nose

mini Oreo

slice in half

dark chocolate frosting

Oreo

circus peanut

small triangles

hat

3 Build snowmen

eyes

nose

arms

M&M mitten

frosting

4 Dress snowman

frosting

fruit leather scarf

frosting

mini M&M buttons

205

SKATING ON THIN ICE!

mini Oreo

Oreo

melted marshmallow

mini M&M

marshmallow

dark chocolate frosting

pretzel sticks

circus peanut

Oreos

Fruit by the Foot

frosting

circus peanuts

pearls

frosting

MELTED SNOWMEN

12 spice cupcakes, chilled
12 Oreos
½ cup dark chocolate frosting
1 (16-ounce) can vanilla frosting
12 Oreo Minis
24 marshmallows
24 thin pretzel sticks
2 circus peanuts
¼ cup M&M's Minis

1. Separate the large Oreos—remove and discard the creme—to make 24 cookies. Spoon the dark chocolate into a zip-top bag and ½ cup of the vanilla frosting into a separate bag. Snip a very small corner from the bag of chocolate frosting. Pipe a dot of dark chocolate frosting on top of 12 of the cookies. Add a whole mini Oreo on top, pressing into the frosting to secure to make the hats.

2. Spread some of the remaining vanilla frosting on top of the cupcakes and smooth. For the melted bodies, place the remaining 12 cookies on a sheet of waxed paper and top each with a whole marshmallow, flat-side down. (Place the 12 extra marshmallows on the waxed paper to the side.) Microwave one cookie-marshmallow assembly at a time for 3 to 7 seconds, until the marshmallow just begins to expand on the cookie. Remove from the microwave and quickly press one of the extra marshmallows, on its side, into the expanded marshmallow. (The heated marshmallow will puff up into a melted snowball shape.)

3. Transfer each melted body to a frosted cupcake, allowing the melted marshmallows to slump onto the cupcake. (Each snowman will melt into a unique shape.)

4. For the arms, trim ½ to ¾ inch from one end of each pretzel stick and discard. Insert the cut ends of 2 pretzels into each melted marshmallow, on either side of the head. Pipe dark chocolate frosting eyes. Snip ½-inch triangles from the circus peanuts to make the noses. Snip a very small corner from the bag of vanilla frosting. Use dots of vanilla frosting to attach a cookie hat, nose, and mini M&M buttons in varied positions to look like they are melting off the snowmen.

Makes 12 cupcakes

1

Top hat

separate Oreo

remove creme

dark chocolate frosting

mini Oreo

2 Melt snowballs

marshmallows

Oreo cookie below

body

head

melt body

quickly add head

3 Add melted snowballs

frosting

cookie underneath

melted marshmallow & head

4 Decorate

dark chocolate frosting eye

mini M&M button

circus peanut nose

pretzel stick arm

209

OREO PENGUINS

12 vanilla cupcakes, chilled
6 circus peanuts
6 inches strawberry fruit leather, such as Fruit by the Foot
12 Oreos
1 (16-ounce) can vanilla frosting
12 thin pretzel sticks
24 black pearls, such as SweetWorks
36 pearlized pearls, any color, such as SweetWorks

1. Place the circus peanuts on their side and cut them into thirds lengthwise. Snip a ½-inch wedge from one rounded corner of each slice to make 12 beaks; set the beaks aside. Roll the slices to make them thin. Cut the slices in half crosswise. Trim the longer sides to taper each piece slightly. Snip 2 small notches from the wide ends to make webbed feet. Cut the fruit leather into ½-inch pieces. Pinch the pieces at the center to make bow ties.

2. Separate the Oreos—remove and discard the creme—to make 24 cookies. For the heads, use a small serrated knife to saw a ½-inch edge from 12 cookies (discard the trimmings). For the wings, saw the remaining cookies in half.

3. Spoon ¼ cup of the frosting into a zip-top bag. Spread a mound of the remaining frosting on top of the cupcakes and smooth. Add the cookie wings, pointed end into the frosting, about 1½ inches apart near the top edge of the cupcakes. (Vary the wing positions to give the penguins character.) Insert a pretzel stick into each cupcake, in between the wings, allowing 1 inch to extend beyond the edge for a head support. Snip a small corner from the bag of frosting and pipe a dot of frosting on the pretzel. Rest a cookie head on each pretzel, pressing the cut edge into the frosting. Add the candy feet to the edge of the cupcakes, opposite the heads, pressing them into the frosting about 1 inch apart.

4. For the eyes, pipe 2 dots of frosting on the head and add the black pearls. Add a dot below the eyes and attach the beak. Add the bow tie to the chin and 3 candy buttons in a line below the bow tie.

Makes 12 cupcakes

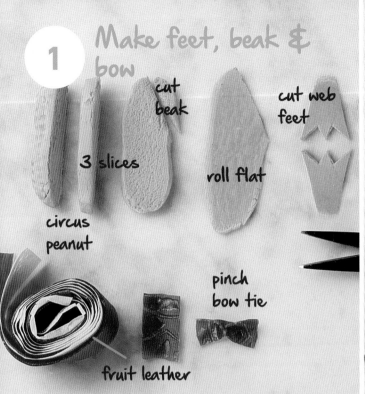

1. Make feet, beak & bow

cut beak

3 slices

roll flat

cut web feet

circus peanut

fruit leather

pinch bow tie

2. Make head & wing

head

Oreo

separate & remove creme

trim & discard

wing

cut in half

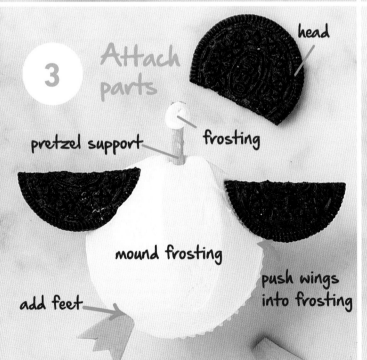

3. Attach parts

head

pretzel support

frosting

mound frosting

add feet

push wings into frosting

4. Add details

pearl eye

frosting

beak

pearl button

bow tie

211

LORNA
DOONEVILLE

nonpareils

sprinkles

sparkling sugar

décors

gum

coconut

frosting

powdered
sugar

White Is the New Sweet!

White candies are a perfect mix with white decorations like sugars, sprinkles, décors, pearls, coconut, and, of course, white frosting!

candy necklace

licorice pastels

Good & Plenty

Canada Mints

candy hearts

jelly beans

Smarties

NECCO wafers

spice drops

Life Savers

Sixlets

Reese's mini peanut butter cups

mini marshmallows

gumdrops

Tic Tacs

Eclipse gum

Chiclets

mini Chiclets

gumballs

mini gumballs

Doublemint gum

mint cremes

mini meringues

Jordan almonds

213

LORNA DOONE COOKIE VILLAGE

12 spice cupcakes, chilled
18 Lorna Doone cookies
½ cup white melting wafers, such as Wilton
1 (16-ounce) can vanilla frosting
White candy décors, such as Cake Mate, or choose an
    option below
2 sticks white gum, such as Doublemint
12 small red sprinkles, such as Wilton
1 cup desiccated coconut
12 thin pretzel sticks

ROOF OPTIONS:

Mini marshmallows, cut in half
White shimmer sugar, such as Cake Mate
White pearls, such as SweetWorks
White nonpareils, such as Wilton
White stick gum, such as Doublemint,
    cut with pinking shears

1. For the roofs, use a small serrated knife to saw 6 of the cookies in half on an angle. Line a cookie sheet with waxed paper. Put the melting wafers in a zip-top bag and microwave in 5-second increments, massaging the bag after each, until smooth. Snip a small corner from the bag. Pipe a line of melted candy along the cut edge of each cookie and press the coated edge into the side of an uncut cookie. Transfer to the lined cookie sheet. Refrigerate until set, about 5 minutes.

2. For the roof decorations, spoon ½ cup of the frosting into a zip-top bag. Snip a small corner from the bag. Pipe lines of frosting on the roofs and shingle the white décors on the cookie roof in slightly overlapping rows. (If using an optional roof candy, make a pattern of your choice.) For the doors, cut the stick gum crosswise into ½-inch pieces. Pipe dots of frosting to attach a door to each house and add a red candy doorknob.

3. Spread a mound of the remaining vanilla frosting on top of the cupcakes, leaving some of the cake exposed, and smooth. Put the coconut in a bowl and roll the tops of the cupcakes in the coconut to coat. Gently pat to reshape. Brush any excess coconut from the cupcake edges.

4. Insert a pretzel stick into the center of each cupcake to support the houses, leaving 1 inch exposed. Pipe a dot of frosting on the tip of the pretzel stick. Add a house to each cupcake, pressing it into the frosting and resting it against the pretzel stick.

Makes 12 cupcakes

214

1 Construct houses

Lorna Doone cookies

melted candy

house

glue roof

cut corner to corner

2 Decorate house

overlap rows

frosting

white décors

sprinkle knob

3 Coconut coat

desiccated coconut

frosting mound

leave edge exposed

4 House raising

frosting

pretzel support

lean house against pretzel

BUGLE TREES

12 spice cupcakes, chilled
36 cone-shaped corn snacks, such as Bugles
½ cup white melting wafers, such as Wilton
24 thin pretzel sticks
¼ cup green decorating sugar, such as Cake Mate
1 (16-ounce) can vanilla frosting
1 cup desiccated coconut

OPTIONAL DECORATIONS:

Powdered sugar
White nonpareils, such as Wilton
Red and yellow sprinkles, such as Wilton

1. Use a small serrated knife to saw the Bugles into a variety of lengths (discard bottom part).
2. Line two cookie sheets with waxed paper. Put the melting wafers in a small bowl and microwave in 5-second increments, stirring after each, until smooth. Dip one end of a pretzel stick in the melted candy and insert the coated tip into the open end of the Bugle. Place the trees on one lined cookie sheet. Refrigerate until set.
3. Spoon the remaining melted candy into a zip-top bag, microwaving the candy for 5 to 10 seconds to soften if necessary. Snip a small corner from the bag. Pipe zigzag lines of the melted candy on the Bugle trees. Sprinkle with green sugar while the candy is still wet. Shake off the excess sugar. Transfer the trees to the second lined cookie sheet. Refrigerate until set.
4. Spread a mound of vanilla frosting on top of the cupcakes, leaving some of the cake exposed, and smooth. Put the coconut in a bowl and roll the tops of the cupcakes in the coconut to coat. Gently pat to reshape. Brush any excess coconut from the cupcake edges. Add 2 or 3 trees of different heights to each cupcake by inserting the pretzel end into the mound of frosting on top. If desired, add powdered sugar, sprinkles, or nonpareils as desired for tree decorations.

Makes 12 cupcakes

1 Cut trees

Bugles

cut different sizes

discard bottoms

2 Tree trunk

insert pretzel

dip end in melted candy

chill until set

3 Tree decorating

melted candy

spoon sugar over wet candy

decorating sugar

4 Plant trees

insert pretzel

vary heights

217

CHAMPAGNE COCKTAILS

12 vanilla cupcakes, chilled
1 (16-ounce) can vanilla frosting
Neon blue food coloring, such as McCormick
4 Twinkies, frozen
4 rolled wafer cookies, such as Pepperidge Farm
4 vanilla wafers
1 cup white melting wafers, such as Wilton
¼ cup white pearlized Sixlets, such as SweetWorks
2 tablespoons white pearls, such as SweetWorks
1 tablespoon white sugar pearls, such as Cake Mate
2 tablespoons white edible glitter, such as Wilton

1. For the flute base, use a small serrated knife to saw ½ inch from one edge of the vanilla wafer. For the stems, saw the rolled wafer cookies in half crosswise. For the flute, remove and discard ½ inch from one short end of the frozen Twinkies to straighten the end. Make a second cut 1½ inches from the trimmed end of each Twinkie. Return the pieces to the freezer.

2. Line a cookie sheet with waxed paper. Put the melting wafers in a bowl and microwave in 5-second increments, stirring after each, until smooth. Insert a toothpick into one end of each rolled wafer cookie and use the toothpick to dip the cookies into the melted candy to coat. Allow the excess candy to drip back into the bowl. Set the coated cookie on the lined cookie sheet. Dip a flat end of each small frozen Twinkie piece about ½ inch into the melted candy and set on the lined pan. Dip the cut vanilla wafers into the melted candy to coat and set on the lined pan as well. Refrigerate until all the parts set, about 5 minutes.

3. Spoon ¼ cup of the frosting into a zip-top bag. Tint the remaining frosting light blue with the food coloring. Spread the top of the cupcakes with the light blue frosting and smooth. To assemble the flutes, place 3 cupcakes in a row on a plate or platter, two of them touching and the third separated by 1 inch. Snip a small corner from the bag of vanilla frosting. Pipe a dot of vanilla frosting at both ends of the large Twinkie pieces and place one on the center cupcake in each row, with the cut end slightly overlapping the adjacent cupcake. Add a small dipped Twinkie piece on the adjacent cupcakes, cut end to cut end with the larger Twinkie piece, pressing into the dot of frosting to secure. Press a stem cookie into the dot of frosting at the rounded end of each flute and balance the opposite end of the cookie on the separated cupcake. Press the cut edge of a coated vanilla wafer into the frosting at the end of each stem cookie, using a dot of frosting as needed to secure.

4. Use vanilla frosting to attach bubbles to each flute: a row of sprinkles rising from the bottom; sprinkles and pearls in overflowing drips down the sides; and sprinkles, pearls, and Sixlets bubbling at the top. Scatter glitter and a few sprinkles over the base.

Makes 12 cupcakes

melted candy

Sixlets

pearls

Twinkies

sprinkles

rolled wafer cookie

vanilla wafer

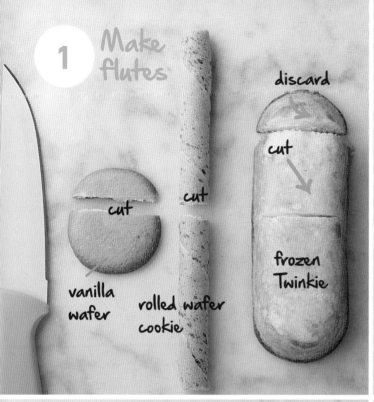

1 Make flutes

discard

cut

frozen Twinkie

cut

cut

vanilla wafer

rolled wafer cookie

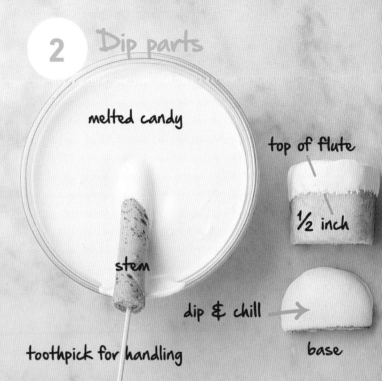

2 Dip parts

melted candy

top of flute

½ inch

stem

dip & chill

toothpick for handling

base

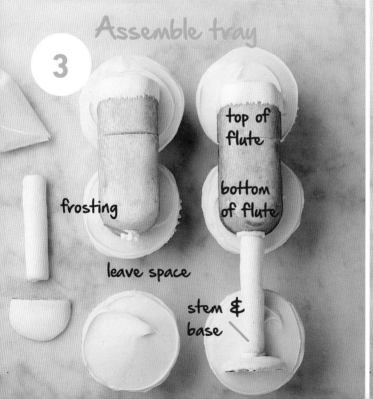

3 Assemble tray

frosting

top of flute

bottom of flute

leave space

stem & base

4 Add bubbly

Sixlets & pearls

sprinkles

edible glitter

attach with frosting

219

CHEERS!

clink! clink!

MAKE IT EASY TIPS
& TOOLS

BAKE IT EASY!

Don't get us wrong, we love Mom's scratch cake as much as the next guy. But we think the fun part is decorating, so we like to keep the baking easy! That's where cake mix comes in. We usually start with French vanilla cake mix because the flavor mixes well with most other flavors, and because the color of the cake is lighter. (Lighter color cake doesn't bleed through liners as much as darker mixes, and it's also easier to create fresh colors when you tint the batter.) To improve the flavor and the texture, we doctor the cake mix with buttermilk: When a mix calls for water, just leave it out and replace the water with an equal amount of buttermilk. Your mix cake will bake up moist and delicious with a perfect crumb. Family and friends will think Mom gave you her recipe!

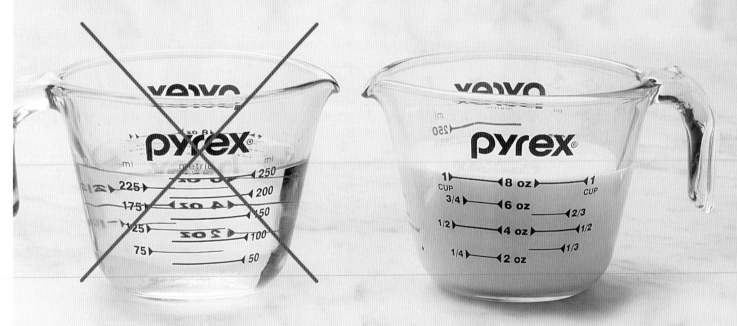

Eliminate the water.   Replace it with buttermilk.

FREEZE IT EASY!

A well-chilled cupcake is easier to handle.

Cool cupcakes completely, then place them in the freezer for at least 30 minutes before decorating.

remove 1 or 2 cupcakes at a time for decorating and keep the rest well-chilled in the freezer

BAG IT EASY!

Zip-top bags work great for piping frosting, and cleanup couldn't be simpler!
Just be sure to use freezer-weight bags to avoid split seams or explosions, and
avoid bags with flat bottoms since they don't have a corner to snip. An easy
way to load a zip-top is to place the bag in a measuring cup or tumbler large
enough to hold the bag open. Fold the edge of the bag over the lip of the cup.
Spoon frosting down into the bottom of the bag. (Be sure to keep the zipper
clean so you can seal it. And don't overfill the bag. It's better to make two
smaller bags than have one that is too full to handle.) Pull the edges of the bag
up and over the frosting. Press out any excess air and seal. Now all you need is
the right-size snip to make a perfect piping bag!

spoon frosting into the opening

fold back the bag to
keep the zipper clean

freezer weight
zip-top bag

measuring cup or tumbler

place frosting in
the bottom of the
bag

1

How big is that cut?

Very small means itty bitty! It takes patience to make a cut this small, but it's worth the effort because this size is great for eyes, nostrils, small dots, and fine lines.

very small

2

A small cut still means tiny, about ⅛ inch. This is the most useful size for adding details. Use it for squiggles, outlines, rickrack, dots, and more.

small

3

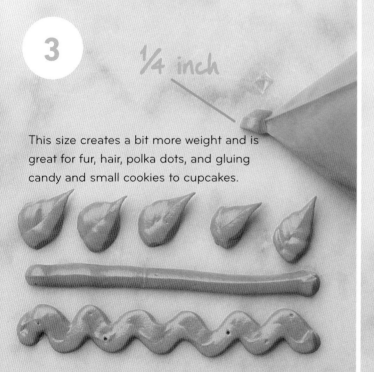

¼ inch

This size creates a bit more weight and is great for fur, hair, polka dots, and gluing candy and small cookies to cupcakes.

4

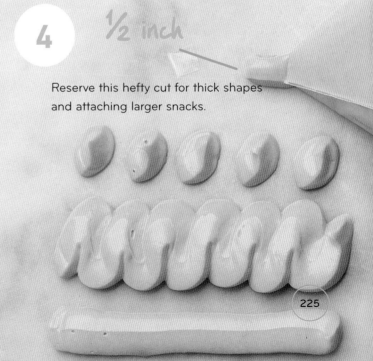

½ inch

Reserve this hefty cut for thick shapes and attaching larger snacks.

EASY TOOLS!

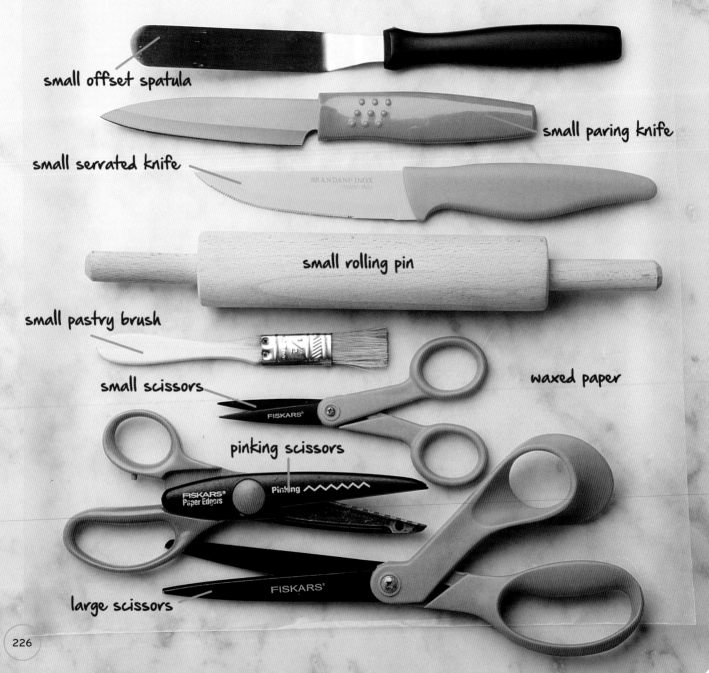

small offset spatula

small paring knife

small serrated knife

small rolling pin

small pastry brush

small scissors

waxed paper

pinking scissors

large scissors

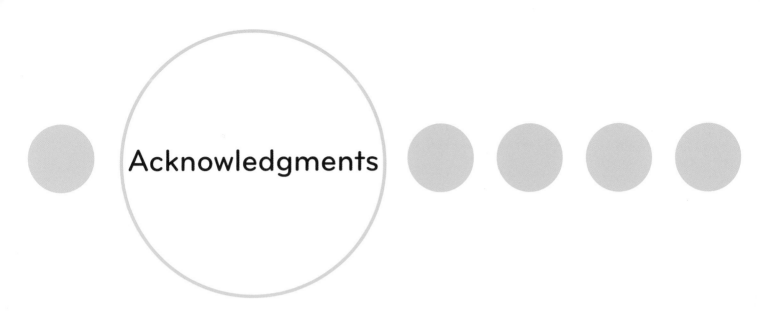

Acknowledgments

Literary agent, Martha Kaplan, is our pillar. Martha handles every kerfuffle with calm authority and then calls us just to see what's baking. She is there for us any time, any day, any meal! More than an agent, Martha is cupcake family!

We are thrilled to be working with a whole new team at St. Martin's Press. They have done a tremendous job helping us create a NEW LOOK for our newest book. Editor BJ Berti appreciated our idiosyncrasies right away. We brought cupcakes to our first meeting and she couldn't wait to eat a Barking Dog! That sealed the deal as far as we were concerned. And BJ brought a top-notch crew to the table. Her assistant, Gwen Hawkes, has done an incredible job tying up our loose ends and keeping us on schedule. It seems like Gwen meets our needs almost before we ask. The design team, headed by James Sinclair, has given us a VISUAL REBOOT. James worked with interior designer Susan Walsh to not only make sense of our cupcake mayhem, but to create an inviting design that we hope has resulted in the easiest-to-follow recipes we've ever published. And the knockout cover treatment by Young Lim puts the perfect candy bow on the package.

You know you've got a good production team when things go right! We have to thank production editor Lisa Davis and production manager Karen Lumley for that. And for a great copy edit, thanks to Ivy McFadden. (We know we've gotten a good edit when they make us sound smart!)

We are extremely grateful to executive editor Elizabeth Beier for her expert guidance. Elizabeth and her assistant, Nicole Williams, graciously embraced us and *Make It Easy, Cupcake!* and made sure we never skipped a beat.

We are really excited to be working with Justine Sha on publicity and Jordan Hanley-Red on marketing. We are thrilled to have their media-savvy guidance.

Back at home, we are really fortunate to have the love and support of our generous families and friends, each a bona fide cupcake cheerleader! We are especially grateful to Larry Frascella, our in-house co-blogger, Cupcake Historian, and general editorial consultant!

And, as always, we thank the makers and bakers of all things sweet. You make our job incredibly fun and EASY!

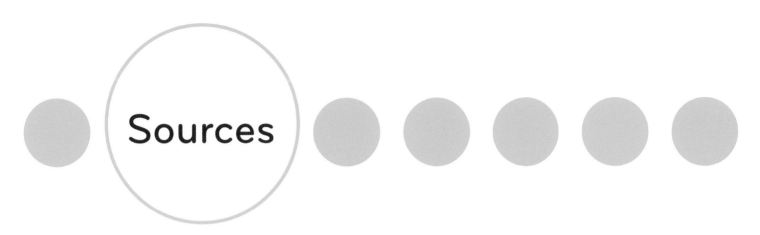

Sources

BAKING & DECORATING SUPPLIES

A.C. MOORE
www.acmore.com
Cake-decorating supplies and crafts
as well as candy and books.

ATECO
(800) 645-7170
www.atecousa.com
Offset spatulas and other decorating tools.

BERYL'S
(800) 488-2749
www.beryls.com
Cupcake liners and as well as many other decorating
supplies.

CONFECTIONERY HOUSE
(518) 279-3179
www.confectioneryhouse.com
Solid color cupcake liners in three sizes. Candy
melting wafers, food coloring, and decorations.

COUNTRY KITCHEN SWEETART
(800) 497-3927
www.countrykitchensa.com
Sanding and coarse decorating sugars. A wide
variety of other decorations including liners, food
coloring, and décors.

DOWNTOWN DOUGH
(262) 299-6038
www.downtowndough.com
Cookie cutters, sprinkles, and decorations.

FANCY FLOURS
www.fancyflours.com
Paper liners, specialty sugars, sprinkles, and
decorations.

HOBBY LOBBY
www.hobbylobby.com

JOANN FABRICS AND CRAFTS
www.joann.com
Cake decorating supplies and crafts
as well as candy and books.

KITCHEN KRAFTS
(563) 535-8000
www.kitchenkrafts.com
Wide variety of decorating supplies.

MICHAELS
www.michaels.com
Cake decorating supplies and crafts
as well as candy and books.

NY CAKE AND BAKING
(800) 942-2539
www.nycake.com
Wide variety of food coloring, candy melting wafers,
sugars, sprinkles, piping tips, and more.

SUGARCRAFT
(855) 867-3635
www.sugarcraft.com
Wide variety of baking and decorating supplies.

WILTON
(800) 794-5866
www.wilton.com
Wide variety of baking supplies, including paper liners,
sugars, sprinkles, candy melting wafers, and more.

CANDY SOURCES

BALBOA CANDY
(949) 673-7021
www.balboacandy.com
Wide variety of candy, specializing in retro candy and
taffies.

BULK CANDY STORE
(561) 540-1600
www.bulkcandystore.com
Wide variety of candies including retro, Kosher, and
colors.

CANDY WAREHOUSE
(310) 343-4099
www.candywarehouse.com
Wide variety of candy. Easy to search database.
Bulk available.

CANDY.COM
(781) 335-2200
www.candy.com
Hard-to-find candies. Search candy by type, color,
event, or party themes.

CANDYALITY
(312) 867-5500
www.candyality.com
Wide variety of candies including retro and bulk
candies in every color.

DYLAN'S CANDY BAR
(866) 939-5267
www.dylanscandybar.com
A wide variety of candy including seasonal offerings.

ECONOMY CANDY
(212) 254-1531
www.economycandy.com
Good source for old-fashioned candy, as well as bulk
purchases.

OLD TIME CANDY
(866) 929-5477
www.oldtimecandy.com
Nostalgic and novelty candies.

PARTY CITY
www.partycity.com
Large variety of colored plastic party decorations.
Candies in bulk.

Index